HELD BY GRACE

BY

CLAUDIA BANNISTER

Ordering Information:

Quantity sales. Special discounts are available on quantity purchases by churches, associations, and others. For details, contact the author at the address below. Orders by trade bookstores and wholesalers. Please email info@heldbygrace.global.

Dedication

This book is dedicated to my two beautiful children,

Marana and Nikio. You both have helped keep my focus on purposeful living, and together we have weathered many storms in this journey of life.

Your love and support enabled me to climb the mountaintop and scour the valley. As we continue to navigate life together, I feel blessed, and I am grateful for the honor bestowed upon me as your mom.

CONTENTS

Foreword

If you are in a valley of indecision about marriage
or a relationship, *Held by Grace* is an excellent read.
It's a story that brings to life God's Grace in the face
of adversity. Claudia and I have been best friends
for more than 23 years, and not only is she an
excellent writer, but I can also testify that she
possesses the ability to minister to hurting women in
a powerful way, she endured many years of private
torture, and now she exercises authority over what
tried to destroy her. Her relationship and obedience
to God was the guiding light as she wrote this book.
As a result, the message in these pages will give
great insight to readers about life's struggles and
victories.

Jacqui Hutchinson,

Founder/CEO

Virtuous Entertainment TV Network
(VETN)

Introduction

There is a gravitational pull in my pages. To say, "I have endured many challenges," would probably be an understatement. Even with this in mind, I don't believe *having many challenges* is a reason for applause or a standing ovation.

We have all been through things, or may presently be experiencing personal trials… I recognized that. However, it is important that we share our stories so that others can understand what kept us going. Our stories may encourage others to *keep going*—even when the feeling of giving up feels like a breath of fresh air while suffocating. For me, I didn't keep going because I felt strong. Instead, what kept me during those tough times was constantly telling myself: *"Claudia, you are stronger than you think."*

It's amazing how those simple words, encouraged me to live more. In other times, they helped me survive. And now, with those words, I have found the courage to share my story with you.

Piecing my life together and finding the courage to write about it has not been easy. It demanded the best of me. When I consider how I've been wronged professionally and personally, it didn't dampen my ambition or my passion for life, when it could have.

Those who know me best, might say that I am "in love" with strength, discipline, and confidence. Somehow—despite everything, I've never quite been like the other girls trying to survive. I knew that I was not just an ordinary girl. From a tender age there was something different about me. During my difficult life experiences, somehow, I always tapped into a strength that I did not know existed until I needed it. I understood that every person has a legacy and impact on the world; and I had every intention of seeing mine through.

I can feel the smirk growing on my face as I write this introduction. It's hard to escape the irony that at times, it felt like my life was directed by Alfred Hitchcock, the famous cinematographer that perfectly captured suspense and horror in his works.

For so long, I thought that the world was not meant for me—that I didn't quite fit in. But as I got older and my faith in God grew, I now know what it means to be *me*. What's more important, I have unapologetically accepted the path set out for me.

I have always believed that each one of us has a specific calling or purpose. For me, regardless of how intimidating discovering ones' calling makes us feel, I am convinced my story has to be one of the reasons I am still here.

Most importantly, for you the reader, it is my sincere hope that my pages bring forth an awareness of your inner strength. I desire this especially for women who have been like candles in windows: Full of light in darkness, filled with endless possibilities, and symbols of safety and hope for the lost and weary. Never change.

Quote: No one is perfect, but you've got to be able to bounce back from your imperfections. You will get there.

Chapter One

I was born and raised in the Caribbean on the beautiful twin island of Trinidad and Tobago—Trinidad, to be exact. My parents, along with my three siblings Eddison, Curtis, Lenore, and I, lived a simple life in a small town west of the capital city of Trinidad.

Before my parents married, they each had a child. My dad had Margaret, his daughter, and my mom had Francis, her son. Margaret and Francis were the first children in the family. Sadly, Francis is now deceased. But when we were teenagers, we all welcomed our adopted baby brother Jason. My parents raised seven children altogether. I always thought that fete was amazing for parents of modest means.

Somehow, even though Trinidad is where I spent most of my life, the beauty of my country still leaves me speechless. I grew up captivated by the sight of lush green mountain tops, colorful chirping birds, and cackling chickens—all of which became an essential part of my childhood.

You could say, the island environment, along with endless beaches truly stole my heart.

My zest for life ultimately comes from Trinidad, my home. I had a happy childhood. Scratch that! I had an incredibly happy childhood! My family was strong, and close—despite my dad being part of Trinidad's drinking culture.

What's more, my mother was a skilled seamstress who'd mastered her craft. She sewed almost anything—from clothing, to household furnishings, if you named it, she could probably make it for you. Still, her passion was sewing bridal dresses. I would watch her as she carefully placed and stitched long fabric and affixed the lace. I remember helping her decorate the trail of the wedding dresses with pearls and other accents—a vivid memory that's stayed with me all these years.

My childhood in Trinidad was a joy. I remember feeling privileged to be surrounded by different ethnicities, as well as, being introduced to a variety of cultural practices and culinary dishes. Trinidad is known around the world for great cuisine and excitement.

Even with all the excitement, some of the best days we had as children were rainy days inside the house. When it rained, the house was filled with the smell of hot-out-the-oven coconut bake. Bake is like bread, but it's not formed as a loaf. The dough is rolled flat and baked in a dish or flat baking pan.

The melted butter ran down our fingers as we took each bite paired with a soft slice of New Zealand cheddar cheese. Now, if we were lucky, we'd also have salted fish (buljol) and a cup of hot cocoa, or some bush/herb tea to top it off. And in the absence of a flavored drink, a warm cup of sugar water would suffice. Both of my parents were good cooks, so we always had home-cooked meals. Eating at a restaurant was a rare and special treat for us.

Alas, all the joy, food, and laughter, could not keep us from struggle. We lived in a two-bedroom home, one of which I shared with all my siblings. We had a double-decker bed which my brothers used, and my sisters and I shared a single bed.

I must admit, it was not always fun for all of us to simultaneously share the same space. However, there was one small exception. On Monday nights, after watching *Dark Shadows* with Barnabas Collins, I didn't mind having a sister or two cuddled next to me, or even two annoying brothers in the same room ready to fight off monsters. My siblings *did* have a purpose.

The house itself had most of the amenities you'd expect. We had a small kitchen with a gas stove and a refrigerator, a living/ dining room with a wooden table that seated six, a small sofa set, and a standing black and white television. There was no indoor plumbing, so we would go to the nearby river to bathe on hot sunny days, or fetch water in buckets and add boiling water for a warm late evening bath. When it rained during the daytime, it was the perfect opportunity to take an outdoor shower for as long as the rain lasted.

Life was different, but I wouldn't trade my growing-up experience for the world.

When I became a mom, I took somewhat of a different approach. I did not necessarily raise my children, "by the book." While I believed that I should give them what was instilled in me, such as morals, ethics, and a tight family structure, nevertheless, I thought it would also be a good idea to provide my children with the upbringing that I did not have. I wouldn't call these things worldly…they were just the luxuries I did not have.

For instance, my kids were fortunate to have separate bedrooms and indoor plumbing. They traveled for summer vacations. They were involved in extracurricular activities, and their minds were not occupied with the routine stuff of life—Fetching water from the stream or standpipes.

Actually, for them, the script certainly changed. For my children to better understand me, they will need to read my book. Over the years, I haven't given my children a clear picture of what life was like for me.

They just didn't grow up the way I did. They had to experience it. And so, because of this, their outlook on life cannot be like mine. We live in a different era and even though they had a similar upbringing as it relates to morals, they did not have those experiences like I did.

We all come from different sectors of life; some carry water from a well, while others turn the tap. My children never faced the situations I did. Undoubtedly, I'm sure they had their own choices and challenges, that were different from mine. My point is, that we all must contend with difficult choices in life regardless of background and social status.

Little things, like the way we think about water is vastly different from one generation to the next. I scooped up water and sipped with hands. Whereas my children reached for a glass, turned the tap, and drank. As I write this, I can still remember what the water felt like. And the impact collecting water had.

Life was routine growing up. I want to clarify that in my growing-up experience, the water did not flow from a faucet, we had to fetch water for cooking, cleaning, etc., and sometimes it would come from the spring if there was none in the taps.

We would take our jugs and walk through bamboo patches where there were frogs, snakes, and bugs, to fetch water filtered by rocks and sediment. These were time-consuming chores. There was no flexibility in our schedules because each day was filled with tasks. Furthermore, if the tasks were not done, there were consequences.

It's for this reason, that as a mom, I allowed my children the freedom to explore who they were, and what they wanted to become.

I also provided many opportunities for them to do so. Now, I'm not saying that I did it right all the time, but they got the freedom they needed to expand their perspectives in life.

And even though they developed their uniqueness over the years, our faith never changed. I made sure we attended church as a family because I wanted them to have a relationship with God.

In my household growing up, we were required to do our fair share of hard work and make significant sacrifices, even as kids. My dad made a roster for household chores. This schedule was made mainly for the kitchen chores, because no one volunteered to wash dishes after a meal. There would be pots and pans stacked high that required scrubbing with fiber and what we called red sand or scouring pads (Brillo), if they were available. It was hard work to get those pots shining so mom could see her face reflecting in them (this was her standard of clean). Not to mention wiping down the stove and the outside of the refrigerator, which was also part of kitchen duty.

My brothers fetched water from the standpipes or the spring for drinking and cooking. No one was exempted from doing chores, my mom even gave me small plastic bottles with handles, so my little hands could help my siblings.

They used buckets to fetch water from the nearby river or standpipe, which made me realize my contribution to doing chores was just as valuable even though I was the youngest child.

Although modern conveniences were limited when I was growing up, I had a family network. Looking back on my foundational years and upbringing, the nurturing I received from my parents helped shape who I am as an adult. Family is the powerhouse in my book.

Even though we lived a somewhat balanced life, Sunday school and church activities took the spotlight. My mother steadfastly instilled morals, sparing no opportunity to ensure that she executed Proverbs chapter 22:6 well:

Train up a child in the way he should grow, and when he is old, he will not depart from it. (KJV).

We were incredibly involved in church activities. There were sporting activities, Easter and Christmas concerts and our summer vacations were memorable. Although we could not afford to travel or go on trips like other families, the fact that we were on a break from school and with extended family was enough. And we looked forward to it.

At times we went to the home of a godparent or another family home or they came to our house, but either way, we had lots of fun. Days were well-organized, and doing household chores was a priority before we could go outside to play.

Now, playtime in my day involved running barefoot on paved concrete or asphalt. We raced against each other competitively. Can you imagine? We ran on hot asphalt and took our flip-flops off so they would not get ruined? If we had access to a ball, it was cricket time. Without an actual cricket bat, we would get a flat piece of wood or a coconut shrub and use it as a bat. Hopscotch was another famous game that only required a flat stone and some chalk. On sweltering days, we went to the nearby river to catch fish. While we were there, a river bath was predictable.

Exotic fruits were like "fast food" in my country. We picked the fruits and ate them straight from the tree, just like drinking water directly from the stream. My favorite fruit is mango, because there are different species of mangoes to choose from. But they just don't seem to taste as good as they did back in my day.

****

The community where I grew up was loving. I saw my mother's interactions with our neighbors. Whatever she had, she shared— which was just one of her many admirable qualities. Sometimes it was a meal, or to provide accommodation at our home for short or long periods. My mother was known as the shelter woman, and I remain touched by this to this day.

She provided shelter to women in need—especially those who faced domestic violence and needed help to get back on their feet. My mother contributed greatly to the lives of others. No doubt.

I recall those times when we left for school in the morning and returned in the afternoon to meet someone sharing our home. Even with just two-bedrooms, and limited living space, we never frowned at her decision to help others—and to me, this was a great honor of our home. The level of hospitality I saw extended to others has truly impacted me. That lesson of hospitality and providing shelter, has stayed with me all my life. As a result, one of the first decisions I made as a young adult was to be hospitable to people without prejudice.

Not too many people have the opportunity to see what true hospitality looks like when they are young beyond immediate family. For me, I had a living example in my mom. And for that, I am eternally grateful. It is because of her love and kindness that my heart is now filled with beautiful memories from childhood of genuinely helping others. There were no expectations, and no need for thanks or praise. Someone needed help, and she was there. My mom was a candle in the window.

****

Growing up, I did not have many friends, but I associated with classmates or brethren at church. I would often invite a friend or a classmate to our home for a meal, a casual chat, or to study. When we were teenagers, my elder brother and I found ourselves extending the same kind of hospitality our mother did. History indeed repeated itself in our generation, and we were blessed that it did.

Thankfully, at that time, we had much more space since additions were made to our home over the years. Eventually, we housed over twenty individuals—including mothers with babies, family, friends, and colleagues, growing up. When people ask, what I loved most about this social aspect of our home, I say: It didn't matter who you were.

You see, at our home, everyone was treated like family!

Quote: Gratitude will make the little you have adequate.

Chapter Two

At fifty-six years old, I can confidently tell you, I've been through it all. When I graduated high school, I was eager to join the corporate world. At the age of eighteen, I secured my first job working as an accounts clerk for a travel service and my salary was five hundred dollars per month. I was delighted to start working and earning my own money, so I could provide for myself and buy those things that I could not afford before joining the working class.

I worked for the travel service a little under a year, then moved on. Soon, I got another job as a store clerk for a music store. There, my salary increased a bit and I was earning seven hundred dollars per month. A definite step up to be so young. Needless to say, I was quite proud of my financial achievement.

For me, coming from rarely seeing or holding money at all, to earning a paycheck felt like grabbing a star from the sky and casually slipping it into my pocket. It truly meant that much to me. But, more than the money, and the independence that came with it, I really enjoyed interacting with the customers.

I was only eighteen years old when I decided to travel to other parts of the world, to eventually become a business owner, and someday get married and raise a family—which was a priority for me. During this season of my life, I was still regularly active in Four Roads Pentecostal Church, the church we attended as children. There, my siblings and I participated in various activities. For me, I especially liked singing in the choir, and to this day, I still enjoy singing.

Every year, Four Roads Pentecostal Church would conduct a crusade within the community. A guest evangelist would be invited, singing groups, and of course, the people in and around the neighborhood. This was considered a big event, and it would usually be held for a week or two.

It was 1982, and during the crusade, twenty-one men and women committed their lives to Christ and also became members of our church. One of the men among them, would become my future husband. This was a pivotal moment for me. Never had so many members joined the church at once—new faces, and friendships. One being my husband. Looking back, it was quite a time for me.

****

As time went by, relationships started forming, proposals were made, and marriages began to take place. There were several weddings from one year to the next, and also there were many cute babies. I was elated seeing the beginning of everyone's lives begin to unfold.

Earlwyn Bannister, was one of the young men that joined the church during the crusade. He lived just down the street from my home, but I never spoke or interacted with him. I actually never noticed him until I saw him at our church. I remember he had a Julie mango tree in his yard, known for being particularly sweet.

One day, a mutual friend at church approached me holding out a mango.

"A secret admirer sent this for you," He said.

Secret admirer? For a few days I lived in suspense wondering who it could be. Somehow, I eventually discovered it was Earlwyn. I saw him at church, and kindly thanked him for the mango. It wasn't long before we started dating.

Our courtship cycle was long, well into seven years before we got married, and this, for the most part, was because we experienced some relational interference. You know the story, people causing petty friction and doubt. After a break, we eventually reconnected and decided being together is what we both truly wanted. In August of 1990, we finally got married.

****

As I write this, emotions are overtaking my words. It's hard to explain, but I believe situations happen in life that compel us to experience different versions of ourselves, and I remember this version of myself quite well. Feelings are often mixed, and to explain them or even to try to explain them, you must first identify the tone and try to understand, why you feel the way you do. This is not easy for most people, and I can only say that at that time, emotions were at their peak.

The time leading up to our wedding was meaningful. I did most of the planning myself, and we were blessed to have help from our family members. As a young woman, I enjoyed event planning (as it's known today), however back then, it was viewed as "assisting" with social events, such as birthday parties, bridal showers, or some Bar-B-Que lime, as we say in Trinidad.

I had a bit of experience helping other brides within our church with color scheme selection, or choosing designs for their wedding party, so it was only natural for me to plan my own wedding. I considered it a hobby, and I enjoyed preparing it very much.

Our wedding did not have a particular theme, but we had vibrant colors of white, peach, and mint green. Our bridal party had twelve individuals; most were family members, a couple of school friends, and church members. The three bridesmaids were my girlfriends, the three groomsmen were from our church, my sister-in-law stood as my maid of honor, my elder brother was the best man, my two nieces were the flower girls, one of my second cousins stood as my mini-bride, and my adopted baby brother was the page boy.

We had two cakes made and decorated by family members, which was a huge blessing gifted to us. Since my fiancé played football, the groom's cake was made and decorated like a football field with a football topper. My cake was a three-tier cake with the old-fashioned bride and groom cake topper, trimmed with peach and white Cala lilies and roses. The ceremony was held at Evangel Temple and the reception at Communication Workers Union Hall on Henry Street in Port of Spain.

****

Twenty-eight days before our wedding, an extraordinary event took place.

The government of Trinidad and Tobago was faced with an attempted Coup d'état.

On the evening of July 27, 1990, I was preparing to go to a marriage counseling session. I was already dressed and primping my hair before leaving the house, and to my great astonishment, I heard an announcement on the television that the government of Trinidad and Tobago had just been overthrown.

"What's happening!" I gasped, trying to catch my breath.

In total shock, I made my way closer to the television. It took me several minutes to process what I heard. I looked to my parents for their reaction, but they were stoic. We all were dumbfounded by what was taking place.

My heart started pounding, and I could feel the change in the atmosphere, not just in our home, but there was an unusual stillness throughout the neighborhood. Suddenly, the sounds of horns, screeching tires, and even gunshots, could be heard in the distance. None of it felt real. It felt like a movie. I picked up the telephone to call my fiancé.

"Hello? Can you hear me?"

"Yes, don't leave the house." He demanded, "Too many cars on the road."

I could hear him pacing—probably trying to get a better view of the street.

He lived near the main road and was quite astonished to see that in a matter of minutes the street became busy as vehicles moved quickly in both directions. Everyone seemed anxious to get to their homes or any place, far from the chaos.

****

Our eyes were glued to the television. The only thing that mattered was trying to figure out what would happen next. My foot tapped uncontrollably as I watched the news and could feel my body tensing up. I rubbed my clammy hands on my lap hoping to wipe away the fear and anxiety I felt. A million thoughts flooded my mind. "Who were these people?" I wondered. "Would they start kicking in doors and killing people?"

Then I thought about my parents and siblings, and how there was nothing I could do to help any of them. I tossed and turned all night, afraid of what tomorrow would bring. It was a difficult time. My mind was exhausted.

The first six days were intense. There was a nationwide shutdown, due to the storming of Parliament and a TV station. The ensuing violence resulted in a state of emergency imposed on July 28th. When all was said and done, approximately twenty-four people died, and many more were injured.

Prime Minister Robinson and other cabinet ministers were held hostage for several days and eventually released. Nevertheless, savagery and looting erupted in Port of Spain, the capital city of Trinidad.

The days ahead looked grim. By the tenth day, everything seemed uncertain about the state of the country and my wedding.

"You both look so drawn—it's your wedding." My future mother-in-law said. "You cannot afford not to look good…"

It seemed like I was stuck in time, while everyone seemed to be moving forward around me. Friends and family were continuing with preparations. Even my fiancé seemed to be less concerned about the state of our country as time went by. Still, all I could think about was the possibility of canceled flights and the absence of essential items such as the dinnerware, cutlery, and wedding favors scheduled to arrive with family members who were coming from the United States. I kept thinking, the political crisis could impede everything.

I was completely overwhelmed, and quite sad, just days before I was to marry. "Was this a sign?" I wondered. I asked myself the same question several times: Why a coup had to happen before *my* wedding?

My mother-in-laws words about "not looking good" came back to me. I didn't want this situation to get the best of me, or ruin what I hoped to be the happiest day of my life. So, after careful consideration, weighing every option imaginable, I came to the dreadful conclusion we may have to postpone the wedding.

It wasn't long before I snapped out of my depression. Thank God we began to see the light at the end of the tunnel! Even though the government enforced an eighteen-hour-a-day curfew, I started believing that there was still a chance we could make the wedding happen—but we had to be on an insanely strict schedule to get things done.

****

The weekend before our wedding, it was finally time to pick up family members. Neither my fiancé nor I owned a vehicle, so my eldest brother, Eddison, faithfully helped us transport our out-of-town guests. The drive to Piarco International Airport from where we lived was approximately thirty minutes or so, but it seemed like an eternity on that day.

The drive to the airport was an unwanted reminder of the terrifying episode we endured just weeks prior. The streets looked unkept, and the atmosphere felt gloomy and rundown—despite the sun shining. National Security personnel was patrolling with semiautomatic rifles slung over their chests. Once again, everything felt like a movie. It didn't feel like my life. And this place…didn't feel like sweet Trinidad, my home.

We finally arrived at the airport, parked the car, and then quickly discovered we weren't allowed inside the waiting area. There were restrictions, and more soldiers with weapons. You could cut the tension with a knife. It was scary.

Finally, my extended family marched through customs without a hitch. I remember giving them long hugs and sincerely thanking them for still coming to celebrate our union, after such devastation. After settling back into the car, almost immediately, the conversation about the coup started. While it was understandable, it still bothered me. I sat quietly and listened when I wanted to shout, "HELLO! I'm getting married! Remember?!"

I certainly didn't want to come off as a "Bridezilla" but every conversation about the coup, was just an unsettling reminder that maybe I should've postponed my wedding.

Would one of the happiest days of my life be forever overshadowed by a failed Coup d'état?

Back home with family, we helped unpacked their luggage, then they settled in, and still, not once did anyone ask about the wedding. As the days progressed, and our big day drew closer, our guests realized why they were in Trinidad. They finally started to inquire about us as a couple, give advice about marriage, and it finally started to feel like I was getting married. It felt real. It started to feel like my life again. I must say…it was nice to be acknowledged.

Quote: Merely being acknowledged is life's wonderful carpet ride.

Chapter Three

Earlwyn was a handsome man. Very attractive, slim built, and stylishly sleek. He was likable, compassionate, and generous. Earlwyn was always willing to help anyone in need, and you could depend on him to diffuse any tense situation with humor. We were compatible. I was gorgeous and fit. I was passionate, resourceful, reliable, and generous—sometimes to my own detriment. We matched.

The wedding ceremony and reception turned out as planned even though we had to observe the curfew restrictions. Nonetheless, we were thrilled to have arrived at this phase. And with bated breath, looked forward to our honeymoon. We could finally get away from it all.

Shortly after the meal was served and the reception ended, we changed into our after-wedding attire. I wore a royal blue and silver bodycon dress that my mother sewed, and my husband wore a pair of trousers with a light blue shirt.

After briefly greeting our guests, and distributing wedding favors, it was time for us to head to the airport.

A dear friend chauffeured us to the airport. While on our way, we could not help but think that the wedding turned out to be nothing short of beautiful. The ride to the airport didn't seem long at all. We were caught up in the moment, gazing lovingly at each other, holding hands, and talking close. We paid no attention to anything around us. We only admired each other with appreciation. The guests were happy, we were happy, and the wedding stress was over.

****

We arrived at Piarco International Airport just in time to check-in for our flight with not a second to spare. We took our luggage out of the car and hastened to the check-in counter, and within five minutes, we boarded the plane. It was now time for our short fifteen-minute plane ride to Tobago, the sister isle of Trinidad.

We held each other's hand throughout the entire flight, and for a brief moment, it occurred to me that I have started a new chapter in my life as someone's wife— Earlwyn's wife.

Although the flight was short, we had time to recall some of our precious courtship memories over seven years. We touched on a bit of everything. I was amazed at how many topics we covered during that window of time. We discussed our courtship and the events leading up to our wedding. You could say, we took a very long stroll down memory lane—first date, first kiss, the times we prayed, and some of the future plans we discussed back then. Those moments were priceless!

When we arrived at the ANR Robinson International Airport, it was raining as we disembarked. There was no covering to get inside the airport. I recall walking down the first step of the aircraft in my stilettos with my overnight kit in hand. I had to run on the tarmac in those shoes.

We laughed running through the rain! It was even funnier to watch me dodge those puddles without breaking an ankle. But not even the weather could dampen my spirits. I was ecstatic just thinking about our first adventure as husband and wife. Once we cleared customs, we took a cab from the airport to our destination.

It took us approximately twenty minutes to get to the guest house where we stayed. It was a beautiful unit located in Scarborough, the capital city of Tobago. Upon arrival, we were greeted by the property manager and were given the keys to our room. As we made our way to the room, I could hear the wind and rain beating on the windowpane. The wind grew more intense and the rain got heavier. The crack of thunder startled me. I felt my husband's hand tighten around mine, then he looked at me and smiled. Blushing, I smiled back. A rainy night with intermittent thunder, was just what we needed to get cozy. There was a beautiful solace in that moment that made me believe everything was right in the world.

The rain brought out our love-soaked hearts.

****

Apart from the weather, we settled in and managed to get a good night's sleep.

"Good morning Mrs. Bannister," Earlwyn whispered playfully for the second time in less than twenty-four hours. I slowly opened my eyes to see his bright eyes and big smile. Apparently, I wasn't dreaming. This was real. The wedding was over, thus beginning our journey as a married couple.

****

We had a great time in Tobago. We stayed in on the first day because of the weather. The other four remaining days were spent doing a bit of sightseeing in the area we visited. We spent time at the beach and enjoyed much of Tobago's cuisine. We dined on a breakfast of fried fish and coconut bake with sliced tomatoes and lettuce on the side. We feasted scrumptiously on the most famous curried crab and dumpling at lunch, and at dinnertime we could not resist the lobster tails and shrimp cocktails that were served on a bed of lettuce.

When it came to desserts, we smothered our favorite scoop of coconut or soursop ice cream. My favorite was the soursop ice cream served with a slice of vanilla or chocolate sponge cake. The food was so good! At times I questioned if we were more interested in the food or each other?

***

After our honeymoon, we returned to Trinidad and settled into our annex constructed at the back of my in-law's house before our wedding.

We knew that this place was just to get us started, but obviously wasn't ideal to raise a family. We looked forward to a great future together, and after several conversations, we considered the option to build our own home as it seemed the most cost-effective thing to do.

By December of 1990, we were pregnant with our first child, Marana. While excited about our new arrival, we were also concerned about our living space. We didn't have much time to worry about living space, because she arrived September of 1991.

As concerned as we were with our living space, things worked out quite well with a few adjustments.

A couple of months later, we secured a parcel of land within the same community located at the top of a hill with an incredible view of the surrounding city. We embarked on building our dream home with ambition and focus. A few short months after acquisition, together the two of us sketched out our perfect home. It wasn't very formal, but we knew what we desired as a couple.

At the time, we did not have much disposable income to build all at once. So as time went by, we built our home one project at a time. Two years passed and while we had the basic structure of the house built; there was much more work to be done to make it livable. We continued with our project planning. Early in our marriage, one of the first big decisions we made, was not to get into debt. At least not yet.

In February of 1993, I was pregnant with our son Nikio, and still we were nowhere close to completing our home. The baby boy arrived in November of 1993. Again, we adjusted our living space to accommodate his arrival. Although we lived in the annex, we had access to the main house, which helped tremendously. As they grew, they gravitated to the larger space and spent most of their waking time between both units. We were also happy to move between both units. How interesting!

****

I never imagined that just five years into our marriage, my husband would fall tragically ill. It all started with persistent back pain.

After visiting several doctors, getting one opinion after another, and taking several medications, he did not seem to be improving. It was months into his illness when he was sent to do imaging studies as he did not show any signs of recovery. While we anxiously awaited the results, I focused on working, taking care of the kids, and ensuring my husband got the medical care he needed. When the day arrived for the results, I unfortunately had to work. So my husband's father accompanied him to the doctor's office. In March of 1995, my husband was diagnosed with cancer.

We prayed and trusted God for his recovery. It was a tough season for my family, but it was devastating for me. With God's help, I managed to get through the first phase of his illness. By August of the same year, his symptoms got progressively worse and he was hospitalized in September for a couple of weeks.

The stress of having to work, take care of the children, and do hospital visits twice a day almost broke me down. A typical day would start at six in the morning. My mother-in-law prepared food and comfort items for me to take to the hospital for him.

I would tidy him and make sure he was okay before I went to work. I worked from 8 am to 4 pm. Every evening when I left the office, I went to the hospital to see him.

Visiting hours lasted for just one hour, but sometimes I would stay a couple of minutes extra to make sure he was doing okay. After my time with him, I went home to take care of the kids. I did this for three weeks, but it felt like three years.

One evening as I climbed those hospital stairs for the hundredth time, I stopped in my tracks. I was almost out of breath, but I wasn't tired. Tears began to well in my eyes and I could feel the emotion taking me over. I couldn't hold it in anymore. I burst into tears. With tears falling from my eyes and rolling down my cheeks, I whispered, "Lord, where are you?"

People were all around, yet in this season, I felt so alone. I took a deep breath then exhaled, "Claudia...you are stronger than you think," I told myself. I forced myself up the last flight of stairs, and before I approached Earlwyn bedside, I dried my tears and consoled myself.

I have never been that person who pretends things are okay, but on this day...I pretended to be strong for my husband. He couldn't see me cry—not this time. I put on the smile he loved so much, and encouraged him to keep the faith and be strong.

"We're going to get through this together, okay?" He smiled gently and held my hand. He seemed reassured, but only God knew how weak I felt as I spoke those words.

After about three or four weeks, Earlwyn was released from the hospital, but it wasn't because he was better. The doctors let him come home, because there was nothing more they could do. The cancer had spread throughout his entire body. Even after hearing the news, and digesting the news...I believed he would live. I simply continued to trust that he would recover. I mean he had to, right? Our lives were just starting, our children were growing, we still had a house to build, we had a whole life to live—together.

My expectations, hopes, and dreams were short-lived as he succumbed to his illness. Regrettably, he passed away six months after his short battle with cancer. I was devastated.

The days leading up to his burial were filled with exhaustion, anxiety, and uncontrollable tears as the reality of his death intensified.

Family and friends were incredibly supportive financially and otherwise. More family came in from the US for the funeral, and some could not make it in on time, but the support I received during this time was a blessing.

The day of his homegoing service arrived. The funeral was held at Diego Martin Pentecostal Church, located at Quarry Street Diego Martin. The church was filled for Earlwyn. Crowds of people stood outside the church building, and on the streets, just to pay their respects. He was well known in the community and in the football arena.

Earlwyn was lovingly called, "the flying Pentecostal." His position on the field during games was goalkeeper. He leapt so high at times to defend the goal, that it kind of looked like he was flying. This ability, in conjunction with his Pentecostal faith, and Earlwyn, "the flying Pentecostal" was born.

He was a passionate player who enjoyed the sport and never missed an opportunity to attend a game.

As I got the kids ready for the service. I pleaded with God to be my strength because whatever strength I *believed* I had progressively diminished as the days went by. The kids were too young to understand what was going on entirely. As I look back, I grieved for three!

As we approached the church, I felt overwhelmed; the grief was unbearable, and I couldn't stop crying. It wasn't easy to contain myself. By this time, my makeup looked a mess, but it did not matter. My husband could not see me anyway. I eventually made it into the church and was seated at the front looking at the casket. My kids sat with me, one on each side. I looked at them as they stared at the coffin, not understanding why mommy was crying.

Suddenly, without questions asked or warning, their aunt took them both, lifted them one at a time to see his body.   My daughter, just two years old, asked, "Why is daddy lying there?"

I had no answer. At least not one that a two-year old would understand at a funeral.   Till this day, I am unable to articulate my feelings about that moment.   How was I going to explain this to her? The truth is, I never tried to until she was much older and could understand. Then, when I explained it to her, I didn't understand any of it myself.

Throughout the years, I did my best to keep the memory of their dad alive. We would look at his pictures and talk about what life would have been if he were here.   I tried extremely hard to stay focused on what life was for us after Earlwyn's passing and remain focused on my obligations as a mom.

Our first Christmas was tough, particularly for me. Nothing seemed to matter. And then, with all the preparations and festivities of the season going on, I did what any parent would do to make their children happy.

I made sure they were well taken care of, ignoring my own grief. On Christmas Eve night, I put the kids to bed, and arranged their presents for when they woke up on Christmas morning. It was a difficult night for me. I got no rest, and was still awake at midnight.

Flashbacks filled my thoughts, remembering our previous Christmas. What seemed like endless memories of the fun times we had as a family. Each thought initiated another sorrowful moment, it seemed never-ending. That night the grief was intense; I cried my eyes out while my kids slept. Somehow, we managed to get through the holiday season and anticipated a fresh start in the New Year.

My efforts to stay optimistic and manage the emotional turmoil tearing me apart took more than anyone can imagine. It was not just willpower or kind words of encouragement but rather deep thoughts of what had happened as I tried to figure out what was next for me as a single parent with two babies.

Months into his passing, I watched my children play and gave great thought to our reality as a family. Agonizingly, and with tears streaming down my face, I asked myself, "How can I do this without you, Earlwyn?"

How would I raise these kids without their father? I had no answers.

The only assurance I had, was God being with us, and the fact that my kids were partly sheltered from the intense grief I continued to experience.

We never got to complete the home we sketched out as newlyweds. My focus then was to provide for the children, so there was no way forward for the house on my own. Sadly, for many years, it stayed untouched and unfinished, until it was eventually sold to a family friend.

Quote: I will find my way if I stay focused on the journey

Chapter Four

Five years passed since my husband died, and a lot changed for us as a family. My children were now six and eight years and were in primary school. To provide the necessities for my kids and ensure that they received a good education, I knew I had to change jobs. I worked for a distribution company that sold lubricants. We sold grease, different oils, and additives.

One of the requirements to be successful at this job, apart from the sales training, was to own or at least have access to a vehicle because there was a lot of travel required. Not knowing how I would achieve this, I pondered my situation as a single mom with two children to raise and decided there was no way with my current earnings that I would have been able to purchase a car. This was another hurdle to cross, and indeed it was a challenge. Without a down payment and by the faithfulness of God, I managed to get a small loan from the bank to buy my first used vehicle.

It was a Hatchback Laser painted in blue with black trimmings. It was nothing fancy, but it did the job. I was relieved that I passed my driving test and purchased a car within a matter of months. The children were equally happy to have a car in the family since they got dropped off and picked up from school. A tad of luxury turned its head in our direction and enhanced our life a bit.

Having a car made me more introspective. A car gave me more independence. I didn't have to ask for rides, or spend hours on a bus. I could get where I needed to go, and that fact alone was so empowering. I could take on the world! It's funny what a four-wheel mobile machine can do to your psyche. Motoring around on the road put a smile on my face for the first time in a long while.

It seemed as though every job I entered had a training duration of two weeks, and then I was released to perform independently. This time was no different.

The training was intense, but as a quick learner with determination to become the best version of myself, I kept going, as did my car. I had found my *driving* self!

There was no denying that driving for me was inspiring and incredibly empowering. I won't say I felt like Queen of the road, but I was Queen of the car!

Two weeks passed, and the training was over. I put together a list of clients and made phone calls to secure appointments to complete my schedule. My job required that I make presentations to sell products. What I enjoyed most about this job was the interaction with clients, and their satisfaction with the solutions offered to their establishment. I never quite saw myself as a salesperson but when I decided to get into sales as a career, I nailed it!

Was it a mindset? Were my abilities finally coming forth? Was it my newfound independence that gave me a fresh outlook on life? I can't say after all these years. All I know is…I felt great.

****

The company I worked for held a sales promotion month and offered bonuses for the sales representative who sold the most products. I was aware that I might not be the best at sales, but I kept my eyes on the prize since I could use that extra money for my children. While it's true that I drove my car wherever it would take me, my *drive* to succeed was inspired by my children. And that has been the story of my life.

Now, all the companies' sales representatives had a particular territory they were responsible for in the company. I segmented my schedule and decided to work one day per week in each area of the region. The idea behind my decision was to have follow-up calls with each client on my list after a presentation. While working this promotion and being out in the field for an entire month, I met a man, whom I'll refer to as D.

I scheduled an appointment to do a presentation on a range of products suited for his company. Back then, D owned an auto-body repair shop. On the day of the presentation, I dropped my kids off at school then drove to his location to do the presentation. When I arrived, I introduced myself.

"Hello, I'm Claudia Bannister. As mentioned in our phone conversation I am here to discuss the challenges you currently face within your operation, and to demonstrate how our products can offer a solution, sounds good?"

I handed him my business card. This guy D was dressed very casually. He wore shorts and a tee-shirt, moccasins on his feet, but was clean-shaven. I was dressed in full corporate attire—a business suit and heels. I felt a bit odd, but I made myself comfortable doing the presentation and discussed his operation and the potential challenges within his business that warranted a solution.

"So, are there any questions? Anything you'd like me to explain in more detail?" I said confidently awaiting his response.

"Oh!" He uttered, clearly caught off guard by now having to direct his attention to something other than me. D took a minute to peruse the materials I handed him one more time, "No, no! Not at all, Ms. Bannister. It all sounds good."

I did a short product demonstration, and closed the sale. Nailed it…again. I was so happy.

****

It was an easy sell, maybe a little *too* easy. I wondered if he was really interested in the product or the saleswoman? I mean…he knew that I would have to make a follow-up call to check on my new client. Was this his way of ensuring we would chat again?

The following week I returned to his place of business to deliver the products. The company's delivery guy usually does deliveries, but I chose to do it since I was going to be in the area. This time the visit was different.

We spoke for a while on business of course, but it got to the point where we deviated, and the conversation was now about each other. He owned an auto body repair shop, so naturally D's eyes glanced at my Hatchback Laser.

"How's that on fuel?" I looked back at it and shrugged, "Not too bad—considering the mileage I put on it every day…"

He smirked. And we both chuckled knowing that I obviously needed a better car.

"Well…I have to get going to my next client."

"Thank you for taking the time to drop off the products." D said, now standing close to me. Our stares lingered. He didn't look away and neither did I. At this point, I was certain my cheeks were reddening, so I turned and headed to the car.

"Oh, one last thing," I said turning back. "If you should have any questions about the product…or need clarification, on anything…give me a call."

He smiled, from what I could tell, blushing a bit himself, "Will do, Ms. Bannister."

****

It was not quite two weeks when I received a call from D inquiring how I was doing. It was approximately five weeks since our first business encounter, but we had been chatting on the phone on and off during this time. None of the calls were about the product.

"May I interest you in an afternoon drive?" Initially, I hesitated but decided it would be a good idea to take a break from my intense schedule and do something different.

Since my husband passed, my life was very routine. Work, church, and home with the children. It was that way for many years, except for those times when my elder brother and family friends would go for long Sunday evening drives to different parts of the country. The children and I would go and that was always fun.

By the time I met D, my children were older and life became more manageable. Nonetheless, there was still a void. All I can say is, a part of me was missing, and no matter how hard I tried to fill that space, it remained empty for a long time.

Honestly, it may still be empty.

I finally agreed to go for the drive with D and we met halfway. I left my car and he drove. It was a cool summer evening. The beautiful sunset reflected on the water of a beach nearby. It was breathtaking. Brilliantly red and orange the sunset in the sky was bold and beautiful. It was as if an orange cast was thrown across the sky stretching out over the earth. We parked the car facing the beach. It was so relaxing. For a moment, it felt like all the cares of life were lifted. D slowly reached for my hand, "Claudia, I'm glad you're here with me."

With genuine feelings of happiness and a comfort I hadn't felt in a long time, I looked back at him and smiled, "Me too."

Who could've predicted that very soon, D would become my second husband.

Quote: Close the chapter of your past, move on and be strong.

Chapter Five

As the weeks went by our conversations were sporadic. D also experienced some relational issues from his childhood which he openly spoke about from the inception of our friendship. He had no relationship with his parents. His mom put him out at the age of 12. Ever since he was young, D had to work and take care of himself. I liked that he was seemingly so open. I was aware that he had a daughter from his previous marriage and was divorced.

As the months went by our conversations became frequent. Back then we used pagers to communicate as mobile phones were not readily available. So, every morning D would send me a page to wish me a good day and add something special to the message that would always put a smile on my face. It felt good. I looked forward to his daily messages, and we became good friends.

About three months into our friendship D wasted no time, he expressed interest in taking our friendship to the next level. I contemplated the request, but at the forefront of my mind was: How might this affect my children? Any decision I made had to be carefully thought out, because it wasn't only about me. Now, part of me was apprehensive about dating or committing to another relationship, but I remembered something my father-in-law said openly during the funeral service of my late husband.

"Claudia, you are young and we expect you to move on with your life." My father-in-law said lovingly. "We give you our consent to have another husband when the time is right."

Even in death there was that deep sense of empathy that emanated throughout the congregation as those words were spoken. At the time, it did not matter to me. I couldn't even envision a life with anyone else. But after a while, I understood why he said it.

Those words left a lasting impression on me, and while I appreciated them, I was still sad it had to be said at all. I wanted my husband with me. He *should've* been with me.

Life felt very unfair.

And so, for the sake of my story here and now, I proclaim myself to be an expert at moving on. I say this because I encountered so many episodes in life where I had to move on. None of it was planned, nor was it pleasant. However, it was necessary.

In the process I sought ways to live again, but there were times that "living" seemed extremely difficult to do. But thank God I survived! The thought of moving on at this point was painfully challenging. I acknowledge, knowing how to move on after the death of my spouse was not something I anticipated. I never thought I would be widowed at the age of thirty, although it took me six years to consider moving on, like most things in life there was no miraculous time frame to bring closure to the grief I experienced after the loss of my husband. Having been through this ordeal, I think I am qualified to say moving on can be a lifelong process. It can take many forms and present many roadblocks, but in the end, only the individual can justify their decision. Perhaps, justify is not the right word. Explaining my decision was not easy and still is not easy. Sorrow makes you rusty. You forget how to help the world around you. I was indeed rusty.

I eventually committed to a relationship with D for a number of reasons. He was kind and he appeared to be thoughtful and genuine. In a previous conversation, D expressed that he was not interested in having any more children and this was another reason I said, yes. The thought of a blended family did not present any reservation on my part because I personally knew of blended families who were happy and fulfilled.

The reality of being a young woman and widowed had me fixated on our future as a family, but D made it quite easy for me to trust the process. Whenever I felt apprehensive about anything, his demonstration of love, care, and concern for my wellbeing, and that of my children, seemed to override my hesitancy. I was okay with him.

One day, I overheard his conversation on the phone. He was telling the caller about me and the about the children. "Yeah! I'll have a son now too," I heard him say.

He had counted my son as his own. I felt so blessed to have someone like him in our lives. I also appreciated that we shared the same faith. More importantly, that we were committed to growing in our relationship with God.

****

We were about six months into the relationship, and I still lived in the annex, but with every passing day, I felt estranged from my mother-in-law due to interpersonal issues that made me uncomfortable. The environment became socially unmanageable, and since I was in a committed relationship with D, the speculations never ended. In reflection, I wished there was a way for discussion about matters of my heart with my mother-in-law, but unfortunately there was no opportunity for me to do so.

It came to a point where my

relationship with her was very strained and somewhat anxiety inducing. After careful deliberation, and being a huge advocate of personal choice, I decided to relocate. Moreover, I still felt that it may be disrespectful to allow D to visit often. With that, I informed her that we were moving.

It was a tough decision to make, and the situation was challenging for so many reasons. It literally broke my heart when I made the decision to move on. While some might say that I "uprooted" my children from their only support system, the mental and emotional stress required that I move out for my own sanity.

D was instrumental in my decision; we moved to a unit which was in close proximity to where he lived at that time. It was partly furnished, and had much more living space than the annex. There was a backyard with a swing—the only thing the kids needed to see to be happy. My children became fast friends with the landlord's twin boys who were also close in age.   Likewise, I was happy that I could see D every day since he lived in the same area.

****

One evening I was at D's business with the children, "I have something to ask you." He said directly.

"Okay…" I responded a bit puzzled and cautious, not quite sure what would follow.

"Are you ready to meet my family?"

Before I responded, I thought to myself: Okay, this is getting serious.   I considered what this step meant to him and our relationship, and I eventually agreed.

The time came for me to meet D's family. My children spent the weekend at their grandmother's house so it was the perfect time to get myself together for the occasion. It was a Saturday evening, D picked me up and as we drove to his house he said things that made me laugh. He could tell I was nervous. When we arrived, the warm reception exceeded my expectations.   Everyone was really nice to me. We talked for the entire evening more about mundane stuff but the interaction was good.

I visited his family at least once a week, and the bond between D's mom, siblings and I, seemed as if I had known them for a long time. I still don't know why I felt this way. Perhaps, I *wanted* to feel this way. Sometimes, we do this when we want to move on. I mean, we come to a point in time when we start wanting different things. We are moved by these kinds of feelings. Moving on is not easy—regardless of the reasoning behind it.

I think it's hard because it has the ability to truly break our hearts. The "what-ifs" and "could-bes" and so forth. I was trying to heal, but was not healed. I *still* am not healed, but I move on despite this.

I was filled with mixed feelings, and I still am. Writing this book has been therapeutic and cathartic, in ways I could never explain. Reading and writing about my feelings has been incredible. I've gotten to know myself so differently. I have learned not to deny my emotions, but to embrace them.

I believe we are supposed to take lessons

away from every situation. We are supposed to learn from them despite all the hurt and agony we have endured. I don't know all the answers to the whys, but I do know that we are all here for a reason—and if understanding ourselves better is part of the reason we are here, writing this book has definitely put me on the road toward doing so.

****

While the children and I enjoyed living at our new location, the yard was not properly maintained. There were chickens and a dog that shared the yard space. Initially, I did not foresee any problems. But, as time went by, I grew frustrated with the chicken and dog poop, even after my conversation with the landlord about the situation, no corrective action was taken. We could no longer endure the stench that emanated from the yard. So after living there for six months, I decided to relocate again. This certainly was not part of my plan when I moved out of the annex. Life is unpredictable—even when things seem to be heading in a positive direction. The unfortunate can still happen.

I dislike moving, but had to muster the courage to relocate again. We moved from the North East of Trinidad, and then settled East of Trinidad.

****

As it turns out, D also knew the landlord of this next apartment as he was one of his clients. It was a lovely two-level apartment building located in a beautiful community. The apartment we moved into was on the first level with parking at the front of the unit which was convenient. I liked the area a lot. The apartment was clean and lovely. The only disadvantage was the traffic we had to endure on a daily basis. We spent more time on the road during our daily commute.

After two months of driving from our new location in Chaguanas to Port of Spain to drop my children off at school, after which I went to work, I became physically fatigued. I repeated this process every day for six months except for when there was a statutory holiday. Apart from the commuting distance, we had to deal with the horrible traffic situation.

I left an hour earlier on mornings to ensure the children got to school on time.

It seemed as though convenience came with a high price. D and I didn't see much of each other on a regular basis. When I arrived home during the evening, there was just enough time to do homework with the children, have dinner, and prepare them for bed. We did not have time to do anything else during the week. I was back to the routine in my life. The children were also exhausted from the long drives and playtime at school. Whenever I anticipated a long day, I would ensure pillows and blankets were in the car.

Amidst everything that transpired, I made sure the relationship between the children and their grandmother was preserved. They spoke on the phone, had weekend visits and once we did not have travel plans, they spent their entire summer vacation with her.

It was eight months living East of Trinidad. Both D and I agreed that this was not working out financially and otherwise, so I decided to move back to my parents' house.

My dad died and my mother was in the US for a couple of months. My second brother and my adopted brother still lived at home so there was more than enough space to accommodate us.

D had not yet met my mother since she was abroad. When she returned he had an unplanned opportunity to meet her. One day we picked her up while on our way from an errand. I was driving and D sat in the front passenger seat. She got into the car because she recognized it was me.

As she entered the car, she said hello to D then asked, "Is this my son-in-law to be?"

"This *is* your son-in-law." D responded. I was surprised by his confident response.

D and I spent a lot of time discussing our goals for the future which included the three children. We began to look at properties for sale but desired a suitable location where we would not have to spend a lot of time on the road during our daily commute. One day I was at D's office (it was mid-morning) and I had no clients to see that early. I relaxed for a bit and read the newspaper. As I browsed through the classifieds section, I stumbled upon an ad for an unfinished house that was for sale and the location was perfect. When we saw each other I immediately brought the ad to his attention. D wasted no time and called. We quickly scheduled an appointment and went to check it out.

It was an unfinished house and land for sale. The property had a great deal of work to do to make it habitable but there was potential.

****

We were excited about the prospect of acquiring this property because we were making plans to get married. He approached the bank and was granted a loan to purchase the property.

I was there for every aspect of the process, he always included me in his decision making and I would be present for meetings or anything that was business related. Whether I played, or did not play an active part in the process, I was always there for moral support.

D purchased the property, and it was

time to draft the deed. We both went to the lawyer's office, the clerk went through the documents and asked if both of our names were going on the deed since we were getting married.

"No, just put my name alone." D said without hesitation.

His response struck me as odd—since we typically discussed major decisions. The moment was surreal for me. I watched him as he continued talking to the law clerk, never even glancing in my direction. I felt miles away, and simply like spectator. I fought back tears, feeling slightly embarrassed, and excluded from the conversation. Was this a sign of things to come? Was he going to become my darling little monster? Was this just the beginning?

Bad vibes were chattering in my ear. I wanted to say, "Well my darling, is there a reason that you don't want me on the deed… too?"

Instead, said nothing—still trying to process what was happening. I was filled with cold fear something wasn't right.

When we left the law office there was no discussion of what transpired, but I would be lying if I said his actions weren't concerning. I never questioned, but rationalized that maybe his decision rested on the fact we were not *yet* married. Nevertheless, I was very puzzled.

The moment soon passed, and I let it go. But, that night it was surely hard to sleep.

Quote: Everything begins with a thought but end with a decision

Chapter Six

We were both very happy about the acquisition of the property, it was a great accomplishment. However, there wasn't much time for celebration, work started almost immediately. The first phase was cleaning and clearing the surroundings bushes and debris around the property.

We spent a considerable amount of time discussing the potential of the property and was very focused on the construction. We had many conversations about the design of the house, color schemes, closet spaces, and furnishings. We literally spent our weekends at the hardware store to see what was currently available. We used our weekend afternoon drives to obtain ideas from other homes that were being constructed in various areas. Our courtship suddenly turned into a housing project. It really was dreadfully funny the way we tried to get ideas.

At times, I wished I could just fetch a pair of scissors and some tape and make the house look all better without the hassle. But of course, that was a dream.

D was the one in charge of the project, but I made myself available whenever needed, and was ready and willing to assist. We shared expenses on the project. He bought the materials, and I paid the workmen or vice versa.

We were razor focused on our construction goals, and meeting these goals often required sacrifice. We found ourselves in a number of stressful situations. Fortunately, we always found a way to overcome those hurdles.

After approximately four months of do -it-yourself work on the property, D moved into the house. D lived at his mother's house and decided to move. He wanted his own space and it was ideal because he eventually moved his business to that location as well. However, I never moved in with him. That has always been my policy, and I stood by my faith. The house was not complete, but it was livable.

We decided it was time to hire

workmen. I contacted my colleague's dad who worked many years in construction. He came on site to see what was required, we negotiated on the price, and just like that the second phase of the project began.

Somehow putting this house together gave me additional confidence in the world around me. Maybe it was negotiating, or pricing materials, or managing tight deadlines, probably a great combination of things. It could have been that it kept both my heart and mind occupied.

It was not just about beautifying the house, but it was also about my life. I was trying to assure myself that really sorrowful things can be changed. It's amazing how difficulty and troubles of all sorts can be handled with a meaningful project and a smile.

I started sleeping more soundly. I began to play hostess to the morning and the sunrise seemed to be a bit more beautiful—as did the cobwebs, the dew, and the yellowing leaf. So, in essence building this house was helping me drown the bombs that was going off in my mind. It seemed to help lull the noises.

****

After months of labour and spending, finally, we saw the light at the end of the tunnel.

It was now time to do the tile work, painting, instillation of cupboards and other fixtures. We spent a lot of time doing the finishing touches. And by the same token, we were also planning our wedding which took place the following year.

I said, "Yes" to marriage again because I wanted a stable life, romance, and a family that stayed together. We got married on April 14, 2001. This time around the wedding was a small intimate affair, with just family and close friends. The ceremony and reception was held at The Villa Maria Inn located in Maracas, Trinidad. A really good friend of mine assisted with the planning and decorations. My colleague who's dad was contracted to build the house, did the cake, and other family members pitched in with the catering, serving, and other aspects of the wedding.

The building project shifted our priorities and we decided to forgo a honeymoon. We were perfectly content moving into our newly built home after the wedding, and finally enjoying our home. But, honeymoons are special. I received a financial gift and thought it would be a nice surprise for D to have an actual honeymoon in Tobago. I know you are probably saying to yourself: Tobago….*again?* Oh, yes, history repeated itself, but this time it was much different.

The evening of April 14th was perfect, the weather was nice and sunny, the minister was on time, the DJ and caterers were in place and there was no coup. Everything seemed picture perfect for the wedding ceremony and reception.

As I write I can still see both our daughters in their lovely pink dresses, and my two nieces were bridesmaids. One wore lilac and the other a mint green. The designs were the same with different colours.

My baby brother Jason and one of my co-workers were the groomsmen, and D's brother was the best man. My dear friend who assisted with most of the planning did her due diligence by standing as my Matron of Honor and my elder brother was the man who gave me away since my dad had passed.

I am unsure what took place, but indeed there was something different. When we exchanged vows I actually shed a tear. At first, I thought I was overjoyed, not knowing I was crying for my own future.

****

When the wedding reception ended, D and I drove back to the house to pick up luggage, we stayed over at the Belair Hotel which was close to Piarco airport as we were flying to Tobago early the next morning. We arrived in Tobago around 8:00 am. Our host picked us up and escorted us to a beautiful place right off the beach. When we arrived at the unit, we had breakfast and settled in. We were both tired and decided to stay in for the morning and maybe go out in the afternoon which did not happen. Like I said, this honeymoon trip was different.

We were in beautiful Tobago for three days but D seemed to be more concerned about the house, and what was happening with his business. Things became a bit tense as we discussed his behavior.

In an attempt to smooth things over and enjoy the short time we had left, we went to a nearby beach within walking distance from where we stayed. We spent the entire day at the beach, but D seemed distant and detached. We started heading back and D finally began to open up.

"Why are we here?" He said completely straight faced.

"It's our honeymoon, D…" I figured stating the obvious would check his attitude. At that point, D continued to express his displeasure with the trip. I was totally astonished by his annoyance. I did not respond. He continued speaking and I listened allowing him to vent whatever stress was contributing to his ungrateful behavior.

We walked for probably another ten minutes or so and I was completely silent. We finally arrived at the unit and I wanted to return home that very night, but I didn't. There was a kitchen in the unit so I made dinner after which D decided to watch a movie and I retired to bed.

Now, this wasn't the picture of newlyweds on a honeymoon. This was more like a couple who had been married for a number of years, and this was just one of many disagreements.

We had one more day left before returning to Trinidad and the host took us to do some site seeing. The site seeing trip lasted about three hours, then we returned to the unit for the rest of the afternoon. While we packed our stuff and organized for our flight back to Trinidad the next morning, D apologized for his behavior.

"I'm sorry for not being myself, I'm just stress out," he said pulling me close. "All of this is nice, but I would have been just as happy heading back home to start our life together."

We embraced each other and committed to our new life as husband and wife. Needless to say, we had a great night.

****

The next morning our host took us to the ANR Robinson airport for our flight back to Trinidad. While things seemed to be a bit better, the three days prior really shocked me.

I couldn't help but remember how D cared for me during our courtship, and then the cold bitter demeanor he displayed in his moment of frustration. Sure he apologized, but I had never seen that from him before. I had always been an authentic human being, who wore my heart on my sleeve. Now that I was married to D, I asked myself, when did things change?

We arrived in Trinidad and were planning to pick up the children who stayed with my girlfriend for the three days. What happened next was equally confusing—that to this day I don't understand.

Not even a moment's rest before D changed into his coverall and went to work like it was an ordinary work day. We JUST got back from our honeymoon and it felt like nothing happened. The so called "honeymoon" was over and it was back to life as usual.

****

The next couple months were challenging but there were good times too. My days were busy adapting to being a wife again and balancing work. We still had stuff to do at the house, like getting furniture for the breakfast nook and living room.

In addition to settling in, D's daughter who previously lived with her grandmother moved in with us for convenience and to bond with her step siblings. We were a blended family now and we had to get comfortable with each other.

After talking with D, I decided to go ahead and furnish the living room, and get another bed for his daughter. I wanted to ensure that she felt a part of the family and was comfortable during the transition. Things were starting to feel normal again.

****

Then, four years into our marriage things seemed to be heading in the wrong direction. During that time, my job was having me complete courses and additional training. This involved evening classes that created some friction between D and I.

One evening I had to do a presentation for a class project. I did very well and was given an award. I was so happy that all my hard work was paying off, and I wanted to share the news with my husband.

"Guess what I got?" I said playfully.

"What...?" He replied, not even attempting to guess and be silly with me. I pulled the certificate with a star prominently placed at the top from behind my back and presented it him. He glanced it over briefly, then turned his attention back to the television, "So what?"

For me, it wasn't just the words, but it was also the smug, dismissive expression on his face. His demeanor was cold and callous, like my educational pursuits were meaningless. He made me feel small. I knew something had to be wrong, but I didn't know what. I just couldn't identify it.

Shortly after that day, D started hanging out more than usual and coming in late. Things were going downhill, but I did not understand why. Even with our communication issues, conflicting schedules, arguments, etc., I was committed to our marriage, and desired to simply work through them. Still believed our hardships were fixable.

***

A friend came to visit and was noticeably impressed by the house. She kept remarking how beautiful it was. I casually said: "You should have seen this place when we bought it"— as a testament to how far we had come…together. When she left, D said to me in these exact words: "Don't ever tell anyone *we* bought this property! I am the one who purchased this property." Can you imagine? I was stunned, disgusted, angered, and hurt all at once.

"Why would you say something like that to me?" I was noticeably upset and demanded an answer. His casual response, may have bothered me more.

"I just don't want you to say that. That's all."

He seemed offended by what I said, but I didn't understand why. We were married! Sure, he paid for the house, but I paid contractors, purchased materials, I furnish the house. I helped make the house a home. And for that I deserved credit.

As time went by, we drifted apart and communicated less. Life became extremely busy for me with work, parent-teachers conferences, extra curricular activities, and all the things that come with being a busy mom.

Additionally, I did the banking and helped D with errands for the business since he now worked from home.

With everything going on I still was a dutiful wife and mother.

Our relationship became mundane. I could sense it, and I'm sure he could too. It was very clear to me that D had moved on without verbally saying so. I trusted God as I usually do and prayed for his intervention, but during this period of time I endured seasons of verbal and emotional abuse. D's behavior gave me the impression that I was living with two individuals in one body. At times, D was the God fearing sweet individual that I married, and at other times he was unrecognizable to me —a total stranger.

In our fifth year of marriage, I was served with divorce papers on my job. After a long battle, in and out of court, the divorce proceedings were over.

However, I need to back up just a little bit, because there were a number of events that led up to our divorce that I must mention. What I'm about to say may sound farfetched or implausible, but these were real events that I personally experienced.

When my relationship with D began to change drastically, I encountered some unusual events that still mystify me to this day.

I woke up one Saturday morning, went to the kitchen to prepare breakfast, and something told me to look around the breakfast nook area. What I saw startled me. It was one of the largest frogs I'd ever seen! Somehow that frog made its way into the house and hid under our computer desk. Initially I was afraid because of the size, but within a couple seconds the fear dissipated. I called out to D and with the same breath, I immediately started praying aloud.

I did wonder how a huge frog entered the house? No doors were open, so I was confused by the possible entry point. Since I already had the kettle on, I contemplated throwing hot water on it. When I turned around, the frog was gone.

On another occasion, the children and I were asleep in my bedroom, when I woke up there was a white frog sitting on top of a television. I wiped my eyes to make sure I wasn't seeing things.

I looked over at the kids who were still asleep. I didn't want to make a commotion, so, again I prayed. Soon after, the frog leaped in the direction of the bedroom window, straight out the gate, never to be seen again.

The event I'm about to describe, may have topped the others. We were living in the same house but separately. I am a firm believer in matrimonial commitment and covenant, because of this, even though our relationship was severely strained, I never stopped wearing my wedding rings.

One day, while at work preparing to leave the office, I used the washroom, washed my hands and powdered my face. While washing my hands my wedding rings were on, I saw them with my own eyes. For whatever it's worth I looked at my hands on the steering wheel and realized that my wedding rings was not on my finger. Yes, that's exactly what I said. My wedding rings disappeared from my fingers!

To this day, I have no idea where they went. But what I do know, there was something rather unusual taking place and had it not been for the grace of God, I would not be here today to tell my story.

Startled and a bit confused, I picked up the children and returned to the office. I looked everywhere possible, my co-workers also helped as they looked around for the rings, but they were never found. Every time I think about this strange occurrence, one word comes to mind: MYSTERY.

****

LIVING HOMELESS AND BEHIND
PLYWOOD

One bright and sunny afternoon, I came home from work. My jaw dropped. The house that I left in the morning was not the house I walked into. I came home to find a section of the house blocked off with plywood.

At first, I thought I entered the wrong house, then, I realized that D had separated himself from me and my children. Crazy. He now occupied the living room and had no interaction whatsoever with us.   He had become horrifically toxic.   But, by this time, it was simply too late.

The situation had imploded.   My children were essentially living with a monster. Unfortunately, I could not shield them the way I wanted.   His bitter contempt for us was a demoralizing battle of wits.

This went on for approximately two or three months. The pettiness and childish behavior from D was a weird experience. Many times it felt like I was watching my own life. Was *this* a movie? This couldn't *really* be happening to me, I thought. We were indeed homeless…in our home.

It was an ironic shot of a house's façade literally falling on life as my children and I knew it.   D radiated with insincerity and it loomed over me like a black cloud.   My emotions seemed tangled in the recovery efforts of my first husband's death and even now it is difficult for me to comprehend my misery. It's still a mystery to me.

****

In the summer of that year, a family member invited the children and me for a vacation since the situation was extremely stressful—not just for me but also the children.

I thought it would be a good break for us, especially for the children. I accepted the invitation and decided we would go for three weeks of their summer vacation. My children were very excited about the trip, but I was not. Actually, I did not feel like traveling, but my family thought it would be a good idea given the situation at hand.

This vacation was most depressing. Understandably, there was this unusual heaviness in my heart the entire time. I tried to enjoy the time away but was once again sorrowful. Simply put, I was anxious.

My anxiety stemmed from my unsettling relationship with D. There was an intangible heaviness dragging me down. Prior to our separation, there was ringing in my head and heart daily, but I tried my best to suppress them, because I wanted everything to work. D was distorting my reality. His actions taught me that life creates more puzzles than it solves. I was getting confused. The ways in which I moved and lived had changed. My spirit was vague and indeterminate. I realized through this ordeal that my freedom from him was essential. He gave me no assurances. No one wants to go through life without meaningful relationships.

I kept trying, and I kept believing that I could turn my relationship with D into a meaningful one, but I was fooling myself. It simply wasn't in the cards. D had to be thrown out of the deck.

Low trust or no trust in a relationship is challenging. As soon as the word "trust" is mentioned, emotions start to rise. Everyone wants to be trusted, but in the end, few are really trusted in life—in their relationships, and marriages. There is always some doubt. I don't like doubt.

The key to addressing a lack of trust in a relationship is to not focus on trust itself, but on the behaviors causing low trust. Had I done this? Had I *really* done this? I wouldn't have put my children or myself behind plywood in a house literally divided. D lived on one side and we lived on the other. I screwed up, and I have to admit it to myself and admit it in my pages. I guess, I wanted to believe in D.

***

It was now time to return to Trinidad, and I began to feel uptight with thoughts of going back to live behind the plywood. When I pulled into the driveway I saw carpet and wood in one section of the driveway. As I parked the car and exited, I noticed that the back door was also broken.

Immediately my thoughts started racing, and I silently questioned if something terrible happened to D while we were away. So, I opened the door and entered with caution.

I was confronted with the sight of destroyed kitchen cupboards, the refrigerator was unplugged, the bedroom carpet was removed, and bare concrete floors exposed. The bedroom door was broken, and the bathroom plumbing destroyed. My home had been trashed. How could someone stoop so low to do this?

"We can't stay here tonight." I said, trying to usher them back outside. I called my elder brother Eddison and told him what happened. He told us to come to his house for the night. Before heading there, I dropped some luggage to the office as it was too many suitcases to take to my brother's house. In the realm of devastation and turmoil, I knew survival was my only option.

****

I prayed on the entire drive to my brother's house and tried to console myself. Only God understood my state of mind.

I felt angry, depressed, and vengeful. So much so, that I hadn't even noticed that I had arrived at my brother's house. I was so out of it. It was almost midnight and the children settled in with their cousins, but I hardly slept a wink. I had no idea how I would maneuver this dilemma. For the second time, my world fell apart. Life was no longer recognizable. It is only now, as I look back, that I realize my lapses in judgment caused my house to be strewn with debris. It is this, on my part, that I find most disheartening.

I laid in bed and all the unexpected tragedies I endured over the years flooded my thoughts. The loss of Earlwyn, the passing of my father, the financial struggles, the chasm between D and I. If my life once again was a movie, the romantic ending surely wasn't mine.

Eventually, D and I no longer associated on any level, and he was out of our lives. Knowing D was nothing more than a disaster. And as I write this, I must admit something that I tried to ignore and deny for so long: D was an imposter—a man I thought I knew. The real D was a monster. I just found out too late.

Quote: Confusion stems from trying to convince your heart of something your mind know is a lie.

Chapter Seven

I never knew how painful divorce was until I experienced it. Being served with divorce papers triggered my past trauma, and all I could thing about was the loss of my beloved late husband Earlywn. I found myself back in a place of intense grief and pain.

When I said "yes" to marriage again, I thought this would be for the rest of our lives. When that trajectory changed, it was traumatizing. The magnitude of separating from someone I loved certainly triggered past distressing experiences. I was thrown into another emotional whirlwind and had no choice but to adapt to a new way of living. While living through all the agonizing stages of the divorce, the intensity of rising emotions ultimately affected me. In an effort to calm those emotions, I went into a state of denial. I denied this situation was actually happening to me. I could not believe it, nor could I accept it. Even though I was blindsided with divorce papers it was difficult to accept that this was my reality. Not to mention the horrifying divorce proceedings. It was a long and drawn out legal process.

Thankfully I had a great support system around me. I had friends that prayerfully and tangibly assisted throughout the divorce, but for me, it was an emotionally lonely journey. There were moments in which I experienced regret and anger, but I never allowed those emotions to turn into hatred and bitterness. There were days when I got out of bed totally depressed and I was physically exhausted by the situation. Those times were what I called my "existing moments". I was existing, but not living. Simply put, life's tragedies seemed unbearable for me and I was just going through the motions. I remember one morning as I woke up, I heard these words emanating from within my heart:

Each day you wake up count it as one day closer to your victory!

Now, at the time I did not fully understand what that meant, how could I? As I looked around, nothing around me looked like "victory." However, as time went by and the divorce proceedings continued. It was encouraging that this long drawn out season was finally coming to a close.

Without having all the details of what was taking place and where our marriage was heading, I did something that could have only been prompted by God.

After dressing for work one morning, I chose red lipstick. I looked in the mirror at my face and pressed my lips together. I paused for a moment and sighed. I opened the lipstick one more time and wrote on the mirror, "I FORGIVE YOU!" I made sure it was visible so D could see it.

He came into the room and saw what I wrote, "Forgive me for what?"

I took a deep breath and exhaled before responding, "For everything!"

He was caught off guard. My sudden compulsion to forgive also caught me off guard. Funny how things happen.

I didn't know why I did it, I just let it all go. Immediately, I felt an overwhelming sense of peace and calm that I hadn't felt in a long time. I believe that was a divine moment of empowerment where I was endowed with Gods grace to release any resentment and anger towards D. It was not easy, but it was the best decision ever.

I realized that my healing and restoration depended on my ability to forgive. What I have learned from this experience is that genuine forgiveness does not deny anger, but it reduces the severity of hurt, anger, stress, and depression I experience. It allowed me to face those negative emotions head on. I desperately needed that.

Forgiveness to me is preserving emotional welfare. It's not just granting pardon to someone who has wronged you. At the end of the day, forgiveness is not for the other person's benefit...it's for your own.

With that said, I forgave D and made peace with the situation. I accepted my reality and trusted God with the process. The moment I did that, I felt hopeful and renewed with a new sense of freedom. Accepting my reality did not mean that all those negative emotions disappeared, because my experience with grief came in waves. But, in essence, there was a flicker of light that illuminated deep inside of me that only I could see. It brought comfort and grace to help me navigate life after divorce.

The funny thing about life is no one really knows what the future holds.

Four years after our divorce I received a text message. To my great surprise it was D. "You are a good woman, I messed up, we got divorced for no reason."

Were my eyes…working? D admitted he was wrong? I could not believe what I read, and actually thought it may have been an impersonator. After finally believing it was him, I smiled and started typing back. "Oh that's funny and it's also too late."

D was suffering from divorce regret. But, I had moved on. I'm good at moving on, remember? I made the decision to focus on my children's education and to fulfill my God given purpose on the earth, and that marriage to D, was a done deal as far as I was concerned.

Quote: Life's difficulties somehow create opportunity to live the life you deserve

Chapter Eight

LIFE AFTER DIVORCE

Some have compared getting a divorce, to grieving a death. In many ways, they are right. The institution of marriage should flow like a brook. It should be filled with energy and love, but when it isn't, it disintegrates and becomes just like death. The only difference for me was that D was still physically alive but, the relationship died. I went through a second phase of grief. I mourned the broken relationship and the good times I once enjoyed with D. A void now existed where there was once affection, conversations, laughter, routine and order. It was difficult.

It was almost two years after the divorce that I fully came to grips with what transpired and felt like myself again. And even though I forgave D, there were episodes where I mentally revisited that painful experience, and when this happened I hurt all over again. Although with the help of God, I recovered from this traumatic experience, the healing process was certainly challenging. It was extremely difficult for me to get motivated about life on my own again. Trying to figure out how to start all over again was challenging and hurtful.

One of the things that contributed to my healing was acceptance. Sometimes we think we are over a situation when we really have not fully dealt with it. For me, it was having the ability to let go of those negative emotions by completely dealing with the true acceptance of my reality. That gave me freedom to move forward, to dream again, and to pursue living again. "Rock bottom" became the catalyst on which I attempted to rebuild my life. I was at the ground floor and had nowhere to go, but up. And with the help of God I did.

I don't think that anyone can ever be prepared for what it *feels* like to be divorced, but I've come to realize that there is life after divorce. Whether messy or friendly, divorces and break-ups take courage. The "post life" requires responsibility and a strong mindset to make it all happen. Apart from God's grace, it requires a substantial amount of positivity, stamina, and personal growth, but it also requires letting go.

What divorce presented to me was choice. I had another opportunity to rediscover myself. Who I am and what I was created to do. I desired to be happy again and not be afraid of the future. That said, I became very involved in church and community activities which were fulfilling. I was in a singing group as a background vocalist and our singing engagements kept me busy as well. Giving service to God and others created a passage for me to be expressive again. I revisited some of those things that were fulfilling. I traveled again, upgraded my professional skills through short courses and even entered bible college to improve my knowledge, and prepare myself for ministry to others. Life seemed to take on a different aura, and the future finally looked brilliant for my children and me.

Moreover, I was part of an intercessory group that met twice monthly for prayer. This was also a major part of my restorative process.

After I graduated from bible college I started to receive invitations to speak at different churches, but particularly women's ministry groups. This confirmed what I believe God was saying to me all this while. There were a number of women with whom I had the pleasure of having conversations about my journey, and for whatever it's worth, there was that one question that was asked repeatedly, "How did you do it?"

People were amazed having heard what I went through, and to see that I was somehow still living in my right mind. My answer has, and will always be "The Grace of God". I say this not because I have mastered the ability to move on, but with each passing day I had to rely on the grace and strength of God to keep moving.

****

I recalled while at bible school I had a communication project to do which required choosing nuggets from different books and writing what I understood from them.

This was no easy project. I searched through the materials that I had, but could not quite get what I was looking for in my resources, so I decided to look elsewhere.

Now, there was this guy who I frequently saw at church, who I will refer to as L. We never had a full conversation, but casually greeted each other at church in passing. I saw him at my cousin's wedding and we had an opportunity for a brief chat. I don't recall what the conversation was about, but we ended up exchanging numbers. Now, at that time I had no intention of dating anyone, it was merely a season of meeting people and expanding my social network.

Our conversations were about work, church, and the mundane things in life. I reached out to him to see if he had any books that I could use for the project and he did. When I picked up the book, the title struck a chord in me, *What every man wants in a woman what every woman wants in a man* written by John

Hagee. The bells started going off in my head needless to say. I certainly was not ready to read a book like this. Nonetheless, I was grateful for the nuggets I was able to extract from the book for my project. Thankfully, I received an "A" on the project.

I returned the book and shared the good news about the grade I received. L congratulated me, then asked what I thought about the book? Now, as mentioned before I was not ready to read that book. My motivation to open the book was for project purposes only. I skimmed through the pages and selected quotes that I had the ability to explain and the rest of the book was untouched.

"I didn't have time to go through the entire book." I said, handing it back to him.

"You should at least read it before you gave it back to me," he insisted.

I was going to respectfully decline, but I reasoned: What's the harm in reading the book?

Maybe there were a few things to learn from it. I took the book again, laid it on the passenger seat, then said goodbye to L.

While driving for some strange reason I struggled with the thought of having to read the book, and be accountable to L for doing so. When I arrived home that evening, I took the book and put it on my nightstand. Ironically, I spent a fair amount of time thinking about it all.

During the course of that same week, I picked up the book several times attempting to read it, but would always be distracted with an assignment or some other priority. The funny thing is I kept hearing those words, "You should at least read the book."

I became inquisitive about the contents of the book, but wondered if L was trying to convey some message that I'd understand after reading the book. Was I crazy? While doing revisions one night, I eventually opened the book, read a couple of chapters, and that was the end of my reading.

In hindsight, I couldn't focus on the book because I was not willing to discover what every man wants—at least, not at that particular time in my life.

I wasn't a difficult person to be around. I've always been an independent thinker. When people are too interested in themselves, they can sometimes think *other* people are egotistical. I never was an egotist. I just began thinking more carefully.

L and I kept in touch, as a matter of fact, we spoke on a regular basis after that book episode.

***

I admired his professionalism and drive as a businessman, but most of all I enjoyed our biblically based conversations. I respected him as a spiritually matured individual and his passion for the things of God. About three or four months into our friendship, a rather strange thing happened repeatedly. Whenever we spoke, for some odd reason and without my knowledge, my phone would call L.

108

Now, some of my friends and my children are very much aware that I am not meticulous when it comes to my mobile phone. It's usually bouncing around with the many contents in my handbag. As a result, when it rings, I'm often scrambling to find it and answer it. It would always be funny to me when L told me I called him, but I never did. I seldom made it a habit to lock my phone after a call, and this would explain why the phone will redial the last person I spoke with. I often wonder who else would have experienced such occurrences. We joked that he *also* attended bible college, because he heard some of the lectures during my accidental calls.

The semester was coming to a close and it was now time for final exams. My days and nights were equally busy. I was overwhelmed by all of life's activities and had little or no time for anything else. Having to work, attend evening classes, assist the children with school assignments, and take care of the home became challenging. I experienced periods of fatigue but kept going as I was already approaching the finish line.

Thankfully, I wrote all the exams and was excited about preparations for graduation. Things felt like they were on the way up. I was on the way up. I felt the positivity. I must admit, going back to school at this phase of my life was not easy. When I considered going into bible school, I did not know how I was going to do it financially and otherwise, but again, faithful God made a way. God kept me and my children through the process and I am grateful! I went into school not knowing what was in the future, but I was confident that my future was in God's hands and that assurance made all the difference.

I believe it was either the day of graduation or the day before. I was not in the field but was in my office. While there, I heard the footsteps of the office manager coming in the direction of my office. In her hands was the most beautiful, breathtaking, attractively designed bouquet of flowers I'd ever seen. She was smiling and so was I. She laid the arrangement on my desk and raised her eyebrows.

"Wow! Thank you!" I said, not knowing if it was from management or someone else. I hurried to read the card. To my surprise, the bouquet was from L. Strange enough, we spoke the night before about the graduation and he offered congrats for making it through bible college with all the odds that were stacked against me. I had no idea this was coming. I was elated. Even though L and I had been communicating for a while, I hesitated to read anything into our friendship. I felt respected and comfortable with him.

Graduation day arrived. L was also invited to the graduation, he showed up, took some photos, and mingled with my family and friends who also attended. After the greeting and photo sessions, L asked if we wanted to have dinner. We agreed, but the restaurant was already closed when we arrived. It was a long day so we decided to do it another time and called it a night.

Quote: An accomplished life is determined by the amount of responsibility one takes.

Chapter Nine

Now that school and graduation were over, my focus shifted to my sixteen year-old son who was preparing for exams the next year. My evenings reverted to picking him up from school and dropping him off at another location for extra classes. Most of the time I would either go back to my office to catch up on work while I waited for him, or used that time to assist my daughter with school projects. I recall one evening while on my way to drop my son off, I received a call from L. What started as a casual evening conversation where we spoke about the kind of day we had, turned into a brief discussion about our life's journey and future aspirations—which I considered to be quite interesting. Needless to say, I appreciated the conversation as it kept me engaged while I waited.

Regardless of the reason for a divorce, lack of trust can shape how we view relationships in general.

This was something I had to deal with. Apart from trusting God, I   started trusting my intuition.

As the months went by my conversations with L intensified. I was comfortable with him and shared the issues of my heart. He proved himself to be a resilient and reliable individual. He gained my respect and trust.

One evening L invited us to dinner. I consulted with my children first and they agreed. We spent the evening at a restaurant and I had an opportunity to observe his interaction with my children. After that occasion, he visited our home. One of the things I admired about L was his spontaneous outlook on life. He had the ability to change what looked like a negative situation into something positive, and it all came together unplanned. I loved this about him.

I believe it was a Tuesday evening when I arrived home early from work. I prepared dinner and took L up on his offer for an evening drive.

This particular evening we drove to a scenic yachting center located in the vicinity where I lived. When we arrived, we parked where we had an amazing view of the yachts. The surrounding waters were calm, but we saw a few capillary waves ripple against the yachts. It was a beautiful sight indeed. The evening was perfect!

The reflection of the setting sun on the blue water was incredibly tranquil and serene. The view definitely created a relaxing atmosphere. We sat in the car and looked on as the wind moved through the water.

Those sights and sounds were therapy for me. I believe it was the same for L. The atmosphere was right for what came next. L expressed his interest and intentions to build a relationship with me. This came as no surprise to me, I knew he was interested, but, what I did not know was how involved his heart was. What I saw though, was his commitment and good intentions towards me and my children. He had an absolute desire when it came to the things of God, which I admired. Every morning as a rule, L called for us to have devotions before we started our day. Our relationship was undeniably different. I was grateful to be in a relationship where there was mutual nurturing of our faith.

When I was asked to commit to a relationship with L, I respectfully told him I needed some time to think about it. Even though I concluded that marriage might not be for me, after my divorce. There were many times I felt like I was robbed of marital bliss.

I spent that weekend at a women's conference. It was a retreat where we spent time away in prayer and fasting. I attended this conference with two classmates from bible college who had previously met L. I prayerfully sought God for his direction. L was aware of my decision that weekend and he also spent time in prayer. All we both desired at this point, was that the will of God would be done in our lives.

L was also divorced as I was and we both had painful experiences. For what it's worth, when I reflect at times, I agree with the statement "misery likes company."

Regardless of how I felt, I wanted to be sure I was making the right decision to get into another committed relationship. After the conference, I felt no apprehension to give L an answer.

When I returned home that Sunday night we discussed how we felt. The feeling was mutual.

One year after that occasion, we went for dinner at a restaurant located at the Yacht Centre, and L proposed to me. Everything in the galaxy was in my heart that night. I was totally surprised! I had no idea that this was part of L's dinner plans. When we arrived at the restaurant, L did what he usually does. He came over to where I sat, opened the car door, made sure I was out safely, and held my hand to support me as I climbed the stairs to the restaurant. He was the perfect gentleman and so endearing. I don't mean to be gushing about him, but he was truly the perfect guy. He was indeed charming. We had a nice quiet dinner, after which we migrated to our usual spot by the water to enjoy the view. It was now habitual.

Although it was nighttime and there was not much to see apart from the reflection of lights on the water, the view was just as beautiful. We stood and looked at the water for a while until I started to get cramps in my toes from the stilettos I wore that night. It was worth it though! We decided to call it a night. On our way back to the car, we walked along a wooden path. As we approached the car L held my hand looked me straight in the eyes.

"You still want to marry me?" The question confused me because I don't recall saying I *wanted* to get married again.

"So, you're asking me to marry…you?"

It was a serious moment, yet funny. We both chuckled. He reached into his pocket and presented me with a beautiful ring.

"Yes!" I gasped. He placed the ring on my finger and we hugged each other for a long time. The world probably turned heart shaped just for us. I wiped a few tears from my eyes thinking about my life then. Apart from being happy there were some deep emotions resurfacing that I did not quite understand.

But it was all good. I felt loved and cherished.

****

Now, I've had marriage proposals before but was never engaged or wore an engagement ring. This was different for me. I remember L and I spoke about this during one of our early conversations. I believe he did this so I can experience what it was like to be engaged before getting married. How sweet! How utterly sweet. I was so very blessed. Not only, was I in love, but I felt a love that took me to the heavens. It was a very unique feeling, and one that I have never known since. It was a moment.

Honestly, it was a moment that had the right emotional component. It was equal and honest—and I was all the better for it. That night I was happy but that happiness began to diminish. I wasn't a newly engaged woman without children. I always had to consider them in any decision I made. I wondered how my children would feel about the proposal? Would they be happy for me? Did they ever even contemplate that L could be my spouse, and their stepfather? This was of great concern for me due to our previous experiences as a family.

When we arrived home that night, L took the lead on this one. He called my children to tell them about the proposal. Now, L and I spoke at length about some of my traumatic encounters so he was very aware of our experiences as a family and sought to establish constancy. Although I accepted, we were both unsure how my now teenaged children would react.

We all sat on the sofa in a circular arrangement facing each other. L and I sat close, but I could feel the anxiety rising.

"Kids, I think it is clear that I love your mother." he said, holding my hand. "And tonight, I asked for her hand in marriage."

I braced myself for my children's reactions. There was a long moment of silence. My children respectfully listened to what he said, but there was no verbal response from either of them. Nervous, I scanned their faces for any sign of happiness or hope. But, all I could see were mixed feelings. I knew they wanted me to be happy again, but they also did not want history to repeat itself.

"Do you have any questions for me...?" L asked trying to break the tension. My daughter leaned forward, "Congratulations!" She said, with a big smile. My son soon followed. Their responses ignited a deep sigh of relief. L pledged his love for us all, and promised to do whatever was necessary to build a solid family structure for all of us. After that there was a strong sense of comfort, peace and a sense of security. The night ended with warm hugs, and smiles, and of course prayer.

****

Now that we had the children on board with our decision we were relieved. The next day L had another phone conversation with my daughter. He reiterated what he expressed the night before.

Being the eldest child, I believe he felt it necessary to alleviate any concerns she may have had with him personally.

To date, I am unsure why he felt the need to do that, but he certainly had his reasons. We were happy to tell family and friends of our engagement, but the responses were interesting.

If anyone had said to me, "You know you are going to get married three times, right?" I would have laughed out loud and kept walking! Not in my wildest dreams did I think I would get married again.

Somehow, as I ponder on this thought, the stark reality of how life progresses continues to remain a mystery—which amplifies the notion that we never know what our future holds. The only consistent thing in life is change. Even with all of this, God is unchangeable! There is no doubt, we all have ideas of what we would like our lives to be. And indeed, many are blessed to say: Life turned out just as envisioned.

For us, everyone seemed really happy about our plans for marriage. For the most part L was respected by my family and those of my inner circle.

Both of our parents were deceased at this point, so we got the blessings of our spiritual leaders our pastors, and we had the blessing of our family members.

Quote: Reality never leaves when mentally tossed away, it changes position

Chapter Ten

The months following our engagement was pleasant. L and I had similar ideas for the wedding, so the planning process was smooth. I had an opportunity to meet his family as he did mine, and the feelings of happiness were mutual. We had gotten everyone's blessing. One can say we were on a path that was quite comfortable for us both. When you encounter this type of unity—being on the same page in a relationship, it puts your mind at ease. When there is no tension or anxiety, somehow the relationship tends to blossom with positivity and accelerated growth. That's exactly what is needed after suffering so much in the past. After so much darkness, I finally believed life was turning around for me. Dare I say, I was happy again?

****

On February 14, 2012 we got married at Crews Inn—our favorite spot. It was a small intimate morning wedding without a wedding party except for my children who signed as our witnesses.

All of our siblings were in attendance along with close friends and family. We had a cake, and the restaurant catered a delectable brunch. As I write this part of the memoir, I reflect on the pleasant memory of my teenaged children signing the paperwork which was truly symbolic of their approval of L. Without hesitation, he graciously accepted the role of husband and dad to my children. The void was filled and my heart was overflowing with gratitude.

Both the ceremony and reception was held at the same location. After the wedding ceremony, we went down by the water for a photo session then returned to the dining hall where we had a short program. There was a total of thirty guests in attendance and it was a delight to see everyone enjoying themselves. It was the perfect intimate wedding not to mention the scrumptious brunch that our guests feasted upon. This added to our joy as a couple. After the ceremonial part of the reception, we changed into travel attire and left for the airport.

I know you are probably wondering about the honeymoon, but let me emphatically state for the record, we did not go to Tobago!

This time L planned a cruise for our honeymoon which we totally enjoyed. It was a great experience. We were on sea for one full week. We visited St. Martin, Turks and Caicos, and St. Thomas. When the cruise concluded, we spent another week in Florida. It was a great getaway and I felt amazing!

I took time to reflect on what I call: "life's chances" during our time at sea. Life certainly changed for us as a family. With L, in many ways, I had finally grown into the person I wanted to be. I was happy. And after a long hiatus, I found *me* again.

****

We returned to Trinidad after our honeymoon trip, refreshed and eager to live out the commitment we made to God, and to each other. I gave up the apartment I was renting, and my children and I moved in with L at his family home which was vacant.

We had plans to purchase our own home within the next year or so, but we also had several discussions about moving to Canada. Since L was a Canadian citizen, he thought it would be a great opportunity for us to migrate as a family.

L had my respect and trust when it came to decision making for the family. I gave it some thought and agreed to make the move. As a matter of fact, I thought it would be great to have a fresh start. We prayed as a family about our decision. It was difficult for us all—particularly the children, having to leave family, friends and the culture we all cherished behind. While it was challenging, we were excited about the prospect. Ultimately, we believed the change would benefit our family.

After nine months corresponding with the Canadian immigration office, we received confirmation that our application was accepted, and a date was given for us to be in Canada as a family. It was certainly a bitter sweet moment. We had no idea things would work out so soon. We had a lot of things to do during the preparation phase. I always thought of moving from one house to the next as an insanely stressful undertaking. There are so many details involved with the process and one can easily become overwhelmed. Migrating to another country compounds those feelings.

As I began to part with valuables accumulated over the years, the reality of moving became insanely real. There were times when those mixed feelings bubbled up again, but I believed they were associated with the move and not our union. I just had to keep thinking of it as packing for a very, very long trip. But, it was not another vacation, it was a brave move.

We worked assiduously to ensure the transition would be a smooth one. However, an unpleasant situation occurred six weeks prior to our scheduled date to leave Trinidad.

****

It was a regular Saturday morning, I was driving to the mall with my children to get something for an event that evening. Earlier that morning I dropped L off to a lecture he had to attend. After which, the children and I proceeded to the mall. Shortly before I reached the intersection to the mall entrance, I waited for the light to change. Suddenly, I heard screeching tires. I couldn't see the car heading in our direction, and in a split second, I felt the impact. The crash catapulted us forward, which caused us to collide with the car directly in front of us. It all happened so quickly. I was shaken. The bang was so loud that my ears popped, and I experienced temporary hearing loss. It was a horrifying moment. I quickly looked back to check on my daughter who sat in the middle of the back seat.

"ARE YOU OKAY???" I screamed reaching for her. She nodded slowly. Then I checked on my son in the front passenger seat and asked the same question with the same intensity. By the grace of God, we were fine. The doors could not open. I frantically kept pulling the car door. We were stuck. I began to hyperventilate, it seemed like I couldn't get enough air! We had to escape from the car, because it was not uncommon for explosions to happen unexpectedly. I began to pray and almost immediately felt a calmness. We managed to climb through one shattered window. Finally, we were safely out of the smashed vehicle. And I could breath again.

L arrived at the scene. After evaluating the damage and acquiring information from the other driver he took us to the hospital for treatment, my son and I were okay—except for the whiplash I sustained. However, my daughter got the worst of it. She had a hairline fracture which required staying off her leg. Her injury could not heal before we left for Canada. Needless to say, she left Trinidad with the use of crutches for support.

As I reflect on this event, my heart is filled with gratitude. God miraculously saved my children from what could have been a fatal car accident. We sustained injuries, but thankfully we all survived. God was with us and with everything that was happening around us, God continued to show himself faithful in our lives. Not knowing what was going to happen with the transition and having to find a job when I got there, I managed to secure a job before migrating to Canada which was also a blessing.

****

In July of 2013, we left for Ontario Canada. It was a midday flight so we arrived around 6:00 – 6:30 PM. We had to get our documentation, so that took another hour or so before we left the airport.

L's sister who resides in Canada, along with her husband met us at the airport and kindly hosted us for a couple days. After which we went to his nephew's home for about two weeks until we were settled in an apartment. After our arrival in Canada, I only had five days rest before I headed to work. Eventually L secured an apartment within the same vicinity where I worked which was convenient. We settled in nicely but took some time to get acclimated. It was certainly a different experience and not without challenges.

L and I were only married for one year when we made the transition. At that time, I was the main source of income while L and the children explored opportunities to study and find suitable jobs. We experienced bouts of happiness, but it turned out that we were not on the same page. We didn't feel unified on aspirations for the future. We didn't discuss our dreams together or how we would finally start to build the comfortable life we wanted. Then it also seemed like we didn't even know how to have a good time together.

Negativity in a marriage creates a chaotic personal life, and that is exactly what I had. I had no issue doing what I did for my family and count it a privilege to be in a position to assist with the financial aspects of the home. What I didn't like or appreciate was being taken for granted.

Still, there were times when endurance was not enough. The new cultural shift and climate presented its own challenges for which I was not accustomed. Apart from this, there was a lack of meaningful and valuable time given to sustain our marriage. There was an abrupt end to the value and time previously given to our relationship, which made me believe I was just a number. My efforts to keep things together were not celebrated.

Clearly, we didn't blaze a trail of unity together. The twinkle of love that I thought was there had vanished into the night a long time ago.

After two years of living in that apartment, we decided it was time to move into a townhouse with more space. In December of 2015, we moved into the townhouse. It was an older style townhome with simple trimmings and most important, a large and comfortable living space. It had three levels.

The basement being partly finished was used as the laundry storage and gym area. The main floor had the kitchen, dining, and living rooms. The kitchen was all white. The cupboards, stove, refrigerator and window blinds were all white. The house had a stylish open concept with wooden floors. Fabric draperies of cream and brown, with a hint of burnt orange. I appreciated having wooden floors, since I prefer large floor rugs instead of having a fully carpeted room. Blinds are my preference over fabric draperies for easy cleaning.

However when we moved to this unit, I used fabric drapes that we had from the previous unit. I have never really understood drapes. There would be layers of fabric when I was growing up dressing the windows of my childhood home, but I never understood it or spent much time on it. Today, I still don't understand the curtains over the windows thing. Personally, window dressing is fashion. Something that is in today and out tomorrow; such is life as we know it.

The windows and the floors were modern interiors as I saw them to be when we moved to Canada. They welcomed us warmly, maybe they were not the height of elegance, but in a way they did say: *Come on in, and sit down, you are indeed home.*

The events of this move will forever be etched in my memory, here's why. The day we moved into the house, it started as a clear beautiful day. The weather report said we were expecting snow the day after the move. However, to our great surprise the snow began to fall on the second trip of the move, and it snowed all day.

Have you ever moved in a house during a heavy snowfall? Well, it was eventful. Talk about a challenge! Thank God the move ended safely. We even threw a few snowballs.

Having moved several times in my life, I came up with a system that I called, "seamless house relocation" —the system worked great for me. This particular move was no different except for the snow. It took me two days to get the house organized and for us to get settled. Having that massive project checked off my list, was a relief!

Life continued and the demands grew with every passing year. Life was hectic for us as a couple. Fortunately, my children were finding their way. L continued to scour the job market, but worked as a photographer whenever work became available. Despite a few hiccups, things were looking up for us as a family, until…I lost my job in 2018.

Prior to losing my job, L spoke to me frankly about job prospects in Canada.

"In this country, people don't do just

one job," He said, being very direct. "And the job you were doing is going nowhere. It's a dead end."

At first, I did not take it personally, but I soon realized that I was being told not to find another job, but to find *two*. On another occasion, during another one of our "career chats" L revealed what he owed on his credit cards. This was a result of his newly found career choice which I knew nothing about. I was concerned about this but assured him that things were going to be alright, not knowing how myself.

I carefully considered ways to help and also weighed my options for another source of income. We had a joint account from which the household expenses were paid, so there were no secrets regarding our balance at any time.

I wanted very much for us to become financially stable, and not live paycheck-to-paycheck. I decided to find a part-time evening job—especially after L told me what his credit card debt was. I sincerely wanted to help alleviate his financial burden so we could spend more time together.   However, this new career choice demanded even more of his time. As a result, the time we used to spend together began to quickly evaporate like water on a hot day.   Our conversations became shorter and infrequent. We were basically operating on opposite shifts. When I left for work, L was in bed. When I returned, he was not at home. This went on for sometime, and this…in my very real experience, was a recipe for disaster.

What was perceived to be the perfect marriage back in Trinidad now sparked concerns. I had a conversation with L back in 2016 to let him know how I was thinking and feeling. We talked things over, and he promised that we would "make time" for one another. To start, we reserved just one day of the week together.   Maybe a night out, or a Sunday evening drive so we could continue cultivating our marriage.

I always viewed marriage as a lifelong commitment, and even being married for a third time didn't change that.

I was intentional about keeping the covenant I made with L and God. I really wanted to do things the *right way*.

Having been a woman on my own for many years, required to make decisions for myself and my children, I believe I did a really good job—despite the setbacks. Now that I was married, I submitted to L, my husband, as the head of our home. I viewed him as the prophet, priest, and king of our home according to scripture. Most importantly, I trusted L and trusted his decisions.

Soon, I began to question his commitment to our marriage because of his actions. There were times I said, "I love you" , and he'd make a funny face, like I wasn't being honest, but then wouldn't say it back. Despite this behavior, I continued to work and perform my wifely duties. Things seemed to be getting better, until December of 2018 when I lost my job.

I will never forget L's reaction when I told him the news. That evening, I saw another side of my husband I never knew existed.

I get the anxiety that comes with trying to figure out what to do next, when the main source of income is gone, but the way he spoke to me was unbelievable. The language I heard spoken by a man that I believed in and trusted, was shocking. He had never spoken to me with such disdain. Had I once again been taken on a ride? Was this another pitfall where I'd have to heal myself…again?

****

An extremely challenging year for us as a family was 2019. After the job loss in December of 2018, I decided I would go back to school to study medical administration. I started school in January of 2019. This was a fast track program so the workload was heavy. I had classes every weekday. When I returned home, I would do my assignments and then, take care of the home. After I prepared dinner, I would put in some extra time studying. I had exams almost weekly or monthly depending on the subject. During this season our relationship continued to decline, I was concerned about our marriage and the direction in which it was heading.

L would usually come in late at nights or in the early hours of the morning, so there was no interaction or conversations. His actions spoke louder than he realized. We shared the same space but there was no meaningful communication between us. As a matter of fact, I hardly saw L.

This situation went on for months and I began to feel overwhelmed all over again. I questioned again, not so much *what* change, but *when* did things change? I still grapple with that thought. But, for some strange reason all during this phase, I kept silent. It wasn't that I didn't want to resolve our issues, there just wasn't anymore fight in me. I grew physically, mentally and emotionally drained of a cycle literally sucking the life out of me. I was out of approaches to this situation, and the times I was able to muster some courage to fight it was futile. Was it fear of the unknown or fear of the inevitable? I still don't know, but I believed being silent was one of the ways I was able to keep my sanity. Exams were approaching and I had to be intentional about staying focused.

I lived for weeks on end with an emotional rock that took residence in the pit of my stomach. Memories of the past resurfaced and again the pain intensified. I became weary. So much was happening at the same time. The situation was always the same—only packaged differently, with new actors. For weeks I contemplated raising the issue with L. Eventually, I found the courage to discuss matters with him. This is where I received more than I bargained for.

Quote: How is it possible to know someone, when people constantly change.

Chapter Eleven

It was a regular Saturday morning and a day in which the course of our lives changed as a family, and one I will never forget. It was August 31, 2019 and I woke up around five o'clock in the morning. I made my way downstairs to my sitting room where I usually spend time in prayer (I call it my quiet place).

As I sat quietly on the sofa I could not help but reflect on my life's journey and the current situation. I tried to pray but could not find the words to express myself. It was an unusual feeling of anguish that brought with it a fountain of involuntary tears. I cried non-stop for almost an hour without being able to pray one word, but I do believe tears are a language that only God understands. I say this because when the tears finally stopped, I gained a strength that I did not experience during this entire ordeal. Having felt the way I did, I decided to approach L regarding the situation. I was a bit nervous, but I believed this was something that I had to do. I returned to our bedroom, and climbed into bed.

"L, we need to talk," I said gently nudging him awake. He sat up and briefly listened to what I had to say.

"We need to talk. What is going on here? Is this a marriage?" I said speaking softly, trying not to wake the children.

Before I could finish, he interjected. "Just so you know, I don't like to feel like a failure. If I had the money I would move out of here."

The statement shocked me.

"WOW! I certainly was not expecting that," I said, trying to keep my voice down.

"Listen, we tried and it did not work, so let's call it quits." He said seemingly unbothered.

"And I have nothing to say to anyone." He uttered.

I felt every blood vessel in my body pulsate. At that moment, I thought about my children, and even though they were adults, I was still concerned about their emotional state. I was reactive. Who wouldn't be? I was about to come face to face with a repeat of the past. I asked L in these exact words, "Can you genuinely say you tried everything possible to save our marriage?" His answer was a resounding "YES." Can you imagine my reaction?

I was shocked and devastated! I started thinking it was me. I started thinking I cannot meet expectations in relationships. I began to wonder about my personality and myself as a person. And then, I realized, this man wasn't right. Life has a way of intruding, but is it for the better or the worse? Perhaps, I wasn't supposed to be with this man. Maybe the page I was on wasn't the page I was supposed to be on.

Life can be so tragic. I kept asking myself: What have I done as a person to endure such heartache? And so, I looked heartache right in the face. I looked at L. I searched his face, every line, every expression, and I searched his eyes. I still could not figure out what was happening.

Every possible emotion in me was churning, but I could not utter a single word. I was frozen. The brokenness I felt was intense, but somehow I reminded myself of all the things I endured because God kept me. With the grace that was available to me, I said these words, "You are a fighter, look at the many things you have overcome, don't give up now. I've discovered one of the hardest lessons in life is letting go, even in the midst of pain.

We discussed his decision briefly. I was still trying to understand him and process what was happening. In less than five minutes, he requested that I call my children in to tell them his decision.

"There is no easy way to say this, but your mother and I have tried, and we made a decision—"

"*We* made a decision?" I interjected, raising my eyebrows. I could not believe what I heard.

He then said, "Your mother is a good woman, and I am a good person. It's just that we tried and it did not work out. I prayed and fasted about this and I think we should go our separate ways."

I was wowed by L's delivery and tone to my children. Apparently, it was all premeditated. He had just been awaiting the right moment. Further, with all the obvious signs of a deteriorating marriage, I was none the wiser. As he spoke, I observed my children's faces—they, too, were expressionless. They both listened to what L said then they politely said, "okay" and returned to their bedrooms.

I might have asked myself a thousand times after that moment, what happened? I chose my peace in the situation, so I did not utter one word. I was not about to trade my peace for a broken person in pieces.

Was I hurt? Of course, I was. However, drama was not worth it. Somehow, I made it through the day, and as evening approached the heaviness intensified. I felt spiritually strong and trusted God to handle the situation, but emotionally and physically, I was a wreck.

That Saturday night L was not at home as usual. I made dinner took care of the house as I normally did then I retired to bed. I was probably asleep for approximately half an hour when L opened the bedroom door, turned the lights on and said, "I'm taking some of my stuff tonight and will pick up the rest during the week."

He wasted no time hastily stuffing garbage bags and whatever bags were available with his things. I laid in bed looking at the time —12:44 pm.

"Where are you going?"

"Does it matter Claudia?"

It dawned on me that this is a situation I had no control over, this was bigger than me. How irresponsible can one be to uproot an entire family from their country, support system, and then abandon them without giving a second thought to this action? There is only one answer to this question. In my opinion, L had emotionally left the relationship long ago, and awaited an opportunity to repeat what I called "learned behavior."

It's said that learned behaviors occur after individuals have experienced, or practice something. That behavior allows the person to be flexible enough to repeat those actions over and over again. In this case, it was very easy for L to abandon his family, since this is not a first time occurrence. Sadly, I never thought this would be my station in life...abandonment.

****

While life presents external and internal stressors from time to time, if partners in a relationship don't share common interests, have compatible work, sleep, or communication schedules, it presents feelings of abandonment. So in hindsight, I was abandoned long before I knew it. Then everything came to a sudden end.

The following Wednesday while I was at school, L came to the house to pick up the rest of his stuff. That week I had two exams scheduled, both were final exams. I recall while doing the second exam I went totally blank. I remember starting the exam, but couldn't concentrate.

All I could think about was what transpired over the weekend. While staring at the paper, tears began to roll down my cheeks. I tried to stop them, but it was another session of involuntary crying.

"Please God I need you right now." I whispered. I tried to constrain myself but it was difficult to do. Students were leaving the exam room and I was still sitting there with tears. My lecturer inquired if I was okay? She thought I was having issues understanding the exam. I explained that it was a personal issue and she patted me on the back. She kindly gave me some water and encouraged me to try my best to finish. Those words resonated loudly within me and I was immediately comforted. I dried my tears and continued to write, finally remembering what I had studied.

With the help of God, I managed to secure an A+ in this exam, and every other exam I wrote. I achieved all A's that semester, and graduated from the program with honors.

I attribute this achievement to God. I moved with a grace that only God can give, I endured and overcame a situation that had the potential to destroy me.

Whether a relationship is over due to death, divorce, or separation, the severity of the pain remains the same. Everyday situations unfold whether it's in our professional or personal lives, but this was phase number three for us as a family. Faced with yet another predicament and not knowing what to say, do, or how to act, made the future look like a giant question mark.

Quote: Don't hide your scars, wear them with honor.

Chapter Twelve

Two years passed since L abandoned the marriage and my efforts to comprehend the reason behind L's actions still astonishes me to this day. Not a day went by where I didn't think about my predicament. But, by God's continued grace, I managed to pick up those broken pieces, and once again…move on.

During this time I focused on a series of mirrored revelations. Meaning, when I began this process, my introspection revealed my weaknesses, as well as, my strengths. It gave me a clearer picture of who I was, and what God has called me to do. It was a teary and painful experience, but most of all enlightening. In the process, resurfaced persistent reminders of failure and heartbreak, while learning to remember all the love and joy.

One of my introspection sessions, reminded me of Jeremiah chapter 29 verse 11 : *"For I know the plans I have for you declares the Lord, plans to prosper you and not to harm you, plans to give you hope and a future."* (NIV)

Since childhood, I knew this verse of scripture, but that day, there was a clarity that in fact, God is the primary architect of my life. He knows what is best for me even when my hopes and dreams fade. It was devastating when my most cherished dreams of having a family that stayed together didn't come to pass and going through various seasons of broken relationships and pain. God still knows what is best for me. His plans for my life supersedes every other plan. This scripture brought an explosion of comfort and peace that was indescribable. I have held to this verse. I have been blessed by the backdrop of God in my life.

As I reflected on the seven years of marriage with L, and his modus operandi, I think it's safe to say that he is someone who also experienced pain as a result of broken relationships—especially divorce, but moved on without being healed from those past traumatic experiences. I cannot be broken by L's issues. He is a broken man. I cannot be influenced by L and his limits, for he has no horizon. I do not know what went wrong, but I do tend to think that L may be running from the fear of commitment. I represented commitment to him and I also represented his fear of it.

In my opinion, there was always that tendency to view our relationship with sentiments of his past. Fragments of those experiences are still alive, so whenever a situation arises, particularly those that resemble a previous encounter, instead of dealing with the situation with an open mind, a stigma is already attached that creates a particular perception. And without professional and personal evaluation of this trend, the tendency to prematurely discard a relationship is a tactic to avoid that imminent pain.

I strongly believe there was a lot going on with L. Things I was not aware of, and this hurts me to this day. I am someone always trying to see the whole of a situation. When I married L, I only got a piece of his truth. It was, unfortunately, all he offered to me. Nevertheless, I have been trying to pick up the pieces. One of the greatest feelings though is that I made my path clear with God and L.

On September 1, 2020, exactly one year after L left, I woke up with an intense urge to send him an email. I wanted to let him know that I forgave him. This took a lot for me. I battled my pride for hours before sending.

What I discovered after sending that email was instant peace. After that day I began to experience the tangible blessings of God in an unusual way—not just me, but also my children. This brings me back to something I mentioned earlier, that forgiveness is not for the other person it's for you.   In my case, forgiveness was for me. Forgiveness gives us a glimpse into life and into God that cannot be described. When we practice forgiveness, it enhances our view of life situations. I started to feel more compassion than anger. Which is ironic having been through so much hurt and pain.

Even though I have been through the rigors of broken relationships, I do not discount the value of those experiences. Every situation presented contributed to a better version of me. I slowly transformed my sense of identity and was intentional about healing and purposeful living. I replaced pity with purpose!

Finding peace, acceptance, and joy again was important because I know if I did not heal, those around me would be gravely affected by my negativity. Healing is what affords me the opportunity to live a more meaningful life. Now, I see a beautiful fulfilled life that I could not have imagined possible. Forgiveness pieced together the shattered mirror. Forgiveness allowed me to see my life's reflection. I am blessed.

Quote: Don't be a prisoner of your broken heart. Forgive, and set yourself free.

****

Despite my negative experiences, I remain a firm believer in the institution of marriage. I respect the covenant made between two people with the expression of vows and applaud those who have stood by their commitment. Marriage is a beautiful thing— when there is true love, not conditional love.

My experiences have often made me question if my relationships with D and L were built on true love or if it was a façade? I think it's a tragedy for anyone to go above and beyond as they did to secure a relationship then at the sight of an issue, the relationship is discarded like a tossed paper bag. Relationships and marriage take commitment and lots of work. Genuine relationships are built on love, but sustaining that love takes effort and sacrifice. Choosing to love your partner should not be an option, it's a commitment that should not be taken lightly. Unfortunately, this is lacking in many relationships today.

I evaluated D and L's behavior from a neutral standpoint. It is my belief, that because both D and L experienced broken relationships —particularly divorce, they had become seasoned to the process. I think it became easier for them to repeat the cycle without remorse.

What was identical in both cases was the absence of a reason for their actions. I must say to date, no formal conversation took place to bring closure to the situations. This is why, much care should be taken when choosing a partner. Marriage is a risk, and it should not be taken lightly. The wrong partner can break your heart, ruin your life, future prospects, and the lives of those who depend on you, and love you.

In my case, I chose men who did not honor their commitment. And who knows the reasons why they did not honor their commitment. My observations have led me to believe that their basic conception of manhood was disrupted in the past or displaced. Simply put, society has made it challenging for men to understand their roles when it comes to family life.

Generations ago, couples honored each other by recognizing their individual contributions within the marriage, but that has drastically changed in our world today. In most cases, men are no longer viewed as the traditional provider, and this can erode a man's confidence.

When I reflect on my situations, I believe the reason for such difficulty, was focusing on the wrong things—their thinking needed to be revamped. If men can sincerely focus on their purpose rather than roles, their actions will flow out of their purpose. If more men believed in honoring their commitments, as well as, honoring love and faithfulness, their souls would be comforted.

Still, people can't give you what they don't have.

Having experienced this lack of reciprocity myself, I know this to be true. From my conversations with others, I realize that it's not just me. Many people have not experienced unconditional love, yet desire unconditional love, without offering unconditional love.

In relationships, we all have expectations, and as much as we would like to think that people generally know how to reciprocate love, this is far from the truth. Not everyone knows how to do so. And, those who may know, have been through disappointment and hurt that still resides in their subconscious. Here, low self-esteem and insecurities, which are detrimental to building and sustaining healthy relationships, enter the picture. There must be a mutual effort for any relationship to work, but I have found that most people already had their fair share of broken relationships and had their love misused and abused. Without being healed, they simply bleed on the person they are trying to love without knowing it. Then they move on to the next and repeat the cycle. Life can quickly become a catch 22.

Experience has taught me that anyone who desires a healthy relationship must understand healthy relationships are built on principles that form the core of healthy interactions. Apart from love, there must be respect, trust, daily communication, and forgiveness. I think there must also be a commitment to relationships, bonding, and humanness.

****

The Do's and Don'ts in Marriage

Don't take your partner for granted. Do not stop courting your partner. Connect every day, make time to communicate, even if it has to be scheduled. Do not go to bed angry when there are disagreements. Instead, seek to resolve those differences and respect each other's opinion on the issue. You can disagree to agree, or *agree* to disagree. When a problem is resolved, don't bring it up when another situation arises. Move on positively, and shift your conversations more toward life and the bigger picture.

Be patient with your partner and always be ready to forgive. Choose your words wisely and think about the consequences of saying the wrong thing. Your partner may rub you the wrong way, but remember why you committed to this person. What made you choose your partner? Is that trait still there? Or does it need to be harnessed? There are green pastures out there, and you can share them together. Life is short. Never forget this. I surely have not.

My personal experiences have also helped me understand what building a life with someone is all about. It has helped me understand what leadership qualities are like in a relationship. It is nice to be with someone that makes you feel safe and secure.

It is all part of growing and mentoring and being in love. Circumstances don't have to be all that glamorous to fall in love, by the way.

You can strike it up with somebody at a grocery store and fall in love with them while waiting in the check-out line. You can be a couple that is extraordinarily private or public with their feelings. There are no *do's and don'ts* in these types of things. Mutual respect is the answer to everything.

Chapter Thirteen

What can I say about love? The first thing I'll say is, I am not a falling-in-love expert, but I have fallen in love, and I do know a thing or two. The swoons of love have been definitive in my life, especially with my first husband. The starry nights watching the stars challenged me. When I have fallen in love, I've embraced it and ridden out the storm, for better and for worse.

Love is great when the sparks are flying, but when the sparks stop...it isn't enjoyable. Love can be quite the heartache. I think about the wrong turns in my life, and they sadden me. I realize, though, that nobody is immune from the losses and challenges we face in life. Life has its ups and downs. It is normal to go through moments that make us happy, and also periods that make us cringe. Love is part of many moments, and love can be beautiful and catastrophic.

****

When you are in love, you don't need to jet-set around the world, wave to a crowd like royalty, or attend big parties and gatherings. When you are in love, you only need each other, kick off your shoes, and enjoy the passion and comfort you both experience from one another. I realize even as a loving couple, you will have your fair share of squabbles. However, you should be able to manage your temper and patch things up with laughter and a few kisses. I do believe this. We live out love in so many different ways. Lifestyles alone can tear couples apart. Still, when you are in love, you must give everything away…your soul, your being, and everything else to make it work. Love is powerful.

Romance blossoms more easily than love. A simple gaze into someone's eyes can do it. But romance must be carried into real life and be incorporated into a relationship. The nature of the soul and love and romance, covers a lot in life—sometimes too much. Someone we love gives us a box of chocolates, and our heart is touched. But, we have to see beyond the gifts, feel beyond the goosebumps, and realize that love must be handled delicately, or otherwise it will vanish and take with it the sparks.

We are held together as humans by the consistency of one voice. That's the voice of our soul. I listen to my voice all the time. Mine is spiritual. God is everything to me. God is how I have made it through love. God was with me every time I had my heart broken.

****

I'm a peaceful person by nature. I want love and romance to work in my life. I love the joy of being in love. Love deserves a round of applause. From love's red-hot romances, to its heart-fluttering sensations, love puts us at the height of personal stardom.

We feel good, look good, and are good when love is acceptable in our world. But, when love's road gets bumpy, it takes a lot of hard work to understand why the beautiful twinkle in our world is dying. We begin to ask ourselves what we did wrong, and when we have no defense for it, love dies, and life changes in so many ways.

There have been some incredible love stories in life, even though each relationship always has its fair share of ups and downs.

Marriages can last as long as there is love. People in loving relationships don't even need to tie the knot to be soulmates. Whether it is a forbidden passion or a devoted partnership, couples find true love or believe they have found true love in the art of attraction and commitment.

****

Still, I believe one of the most important decisions one can make in life is the decision to get married. Even though I think it is a risk to place our lives in the hands of another person, we willingly do it for the sake of love. Everyone wants a happily-ever-after, but not everyone realizes how much effort it takes to keep a marriage from deteriorating. Love in relationships fails as people grow apart; there may be other extenuating circumstances such as debt, sickness, and other relational interference. Once there is no real connection, love quickly exits a relationship. Some individuals get into marriage believing that it is a cure for all their misconceptions, which are met with obscure expectations. However, I think that marriage and relationships fail mainly because of the mere perception of love. People have a basic sense of what love in relationships *should* look like, but love itself is much deeper than our limited awareness.

Love is undeniable and is shared between two people. In relationships, it represents a steadfast commitment to that person. True love supersedes wrong and holds a relationship strong. Where there is true love, one can be their authentic self with limitless expressions of respect, compassion, and kindness. Love will always find a way to communicate its virtue.

During turmoil, morals and values will be aligned with those of your partner to sustain happiness within the relationship because both individuals usually feed off of each other. During the early stages of my husband's illness, a friend came to visit and my son, who was just fourteen months. He kept climbing on me as I sat in a chair. I said, go to your dad and give me a break. My husband responded by saying, "You better get accustomed."

I thought about that recently, seems like his death was inevitable, but it also appeared as if our love was unavoidable. After all these years, I still believe we were meant for each other. I still cannot wrap my mind around why Earlwyn had to leave so early in our marriage? He was an enlightened spirit, a beautiful husband, and a beautiful father.

There was a time when I looked in the mirror and hated what I saw. I felt unloved and ugly. Even though I looked good on the outside, there were a lot of ugly scars inside me. When I started to believe what God thought and said about me through scripture, then and only then, did I live free of other people's perceptions of me. I have learned that I cannot live my life trying to defend other people's thoughts and spoken words about me. It is almost like, I don't care what they have to say about me, as long as, they get my name right!

There is no doubt that I can get down on myself if I believe I have not lived up to my potential. If I look back at love so far, I may still have questions about my love life, and with that comes the questions about life in general. I have learned I must live in the now. I must love in the now because I must never forget who I was before the starry skies and the love-swept moments.

It was always me, and I always had a relationship with dreaming, learning, and just being. My search for the definition of love will continue, and I will have more to share in my many books to come!

There is no better way for me to describe love as written in 1 Corinthians 13: *Love is patient, love is kind. It does not envy, it does not boast, it is not proud. It does not dishonor others, it is not self-seeking, it is not easily angered, and it keeps no record of wrongs. Love does not delight in evil but rejoices with the truth. It always protects, always trusts, always hopes, and always perseveres. Love never fails. People do.*

I suppose I learned what I needed to learn from love and my relationships, and then I usually fixed it so I would move on. I didn't like the guilt of moving away from them. I believe in love, and I believe in loyalty. I have been tinged with anger and overwhelmed by sadness when my marriages have fallen apart for one reason or another. I do think that I have had legitimate cause for bitterness as well. But, I chose to forgive! When something is over, I am left with apprehension, but I am also filled with hope. Love is always around the corner, and hope is always in my heart. Nobody can take that from me.

If there is a lesson here, happiness comes from within. Love is human and delicate. Life is short. The vivid details of love and romance and how I have felt, have filled my heart with joy. Love has been exciting for me and enchanting. I will return to it again the more I think about it with a new sense of understanding. I know in my heart, with all that has happened to me, that I am in love with love! It is what makes me passionate about life.

Chapter Fourteen

I must confess fairness is never far from me. It is never far from my heart. I can hear the whisper of these words reaching out to me every single day. When I allow the word fairness to engulf me in a solitary moment of thought, the word fairness is behind my comfort, inspiration, and joy as a human being. I believe that feeling of justice in life and within yourself (self-justice if you will), is liberating. There is no denying that I've known great heartbreak, and I'm lucky enough to be enjoying some true happiness now.

Sometimes fairness lives a double life, and we get caught in the web of deceit. Unfortunately, life can do this to all living things, and even the fly can get caught in a spider's web. Unsuspecting, we travel into the unknown and look around and wonder where fairness has gone? Rather, where does it even live? I sink into my chair and think about this for a while. It makes me quiet, as I wipe away a new gush of tears. My first husband and I had it all. We had love and fairness, and it was a beautiful package until cancer forced its way into our lives. It spoiled everything.

Cancer stunned me and after all these years, I still have not recovered from how it took my husband away. I still feel confusion after all these years. Needless to say, I am filled with sentimental love and affection. I don't believe my husband's storm will ever pass. Unfairness, can do this to you, and it can make your eyes rest serenely upon life. It is tough when fairness flies away. My husband represented a whole generation of everything good. He just made everything right.

The concept of fairness has me thinking. I could talk for eternity on the unfairness of life and death and everything in between. Mourning, fretting, suffering, complaining, grieving, and so on occupies so many lives. Why? Indeed, the pandemic is not fair. Dying young is not fair, cancer is not fair, and sickness is not fair. So many times, I ask myself what I have done to deserve this and that, and I don't get any answers. As human beings, I don't think we are built for life's unfairness in our path.

Obstacles are unfair. Life is unjust, and I never felt unfairness so intensely as when my husband got sick and eventually passed away. I had young children, and they no longer had a father. We are not built for separation from the living. It is traumatic when we lose a loved one. However, this is all part of life.

Regardless, I pray for a more justly governed world. I pray for honesty and kindness, and love. I pray for all people to take relationships seriously, and to take love seriously and especially marriage seriously. So often written about, fairness has been well described both in prose and in verse, and I feel there is a presumption in me attempting to say anything fresh about it. To be candid, the happiness of many homes is wrecked, and thousands of marriages and relationships are brought to a shameful end because simple fairness has been tossed to the wind. I adamantly feel that in the interests of humanity, fairness must exist for society, and for the world as a whole to exist the way it was intended to be.

Indeed, God's ways are beautiful. The most insignificant acts often bring about the most mighty results and changes on this earth. We must be patient.

There are so many things we just aren't meant to understand. Maybe, it is part of the plan. I just really don't know what to think. I wrestle with this thought often.

Still, I remain hopeful that fairness will come to us all, one day!

Chapter Fifteen

Aren't we here to make a career out of marriage? What happened to love, honor, and loyalty? Why is it so challenging to try to make something...work?

Marriage is a lot of things, but it may be a sign of the times that marriage has become a sea of opinions. It is a place of employment, disgruntlement, politics, social issues, personal statements, and external issues. Marriage and its commitment to it, is not *something* to give up on in my book. It is a succession of lessons.

Together we shape identities, immerse ourselves in situations and conquer the obstacles while keeping our individuality. The married partnership is an understanding that pushes us into a new kind of life and it is the epitome of togetherness. It is an artistic creation of cosmic forces, human choice, and love. Perhaps there is a divine plan to it. I have often wondered if we marry who we do for a reason.

I am still thinking about this one, and I believe I will continue to think about this one throughout my life.

But, decades ago, couples shared mutual opinions and worked as a team, today not so much. Today's marriages have more than a sprinkling of infidelity. Today, marriages have different standards and norms, but it's not always the case.

It is not easy for couples to marry and stay married. Living in the spotlight has never made relationships easy, and many famous Hollywood couples are proof of that. Everyday, it seems teams are under the spotlight. Despite the obstacles, many Old Hollywood couples defied the odds and were able to find true love. Not all of them had a happily-ever-after, but that doesn't mean their relationships were any less romantic.

Partnerships are formed when there is an agreement or commitment. A true partnership is where a couple has shared ambitions and is fully engaged, working toward mutual goals within relationships or marriage. In other words, they are on the same page. But the page turns for various reasons, and commitments fly off the page, which closes the book for many, for good.

I have realized that partnerships are not about the chemistry that brings two people together but rather the emotional integrity and bond that drives the relationship. The love seems more substantial, and there is a sense of stability when there is a duty to live up to marriage. Today, I believe this duty to marriage and the vows we take has dwindled. I am very sorry that this has happened. Marriage has been marred and challenged by extra-marital romance and affairs and volatile behavior for centuries. There are consequences to the marriage partnership. Marriage, life partnerships, and divorces shape society and create society. People today should have increased confidence in their partnerships. They should feel a sense of warmth and comfort, but instead, people are reserved about them and a bit fearful.

As I walk the streets in my daily life, shopping, working, and so forth, I think a lot about today's world. I feel a breeze play upon my cheeks as I think about my life and all I have been through as a person, I remain inspired by my dreams.

I try in vain to persuade myself that desolation is never the answer, but still, it ever presents itself in my imagination as the region of beauty and delight. Why? It's a safety zone where you cannot be hurt by a partnership. However, one cannot skirt the horizon throughout their life. We cannot always sail over a calm sea, but I want to so much. Broken partnerships are horrible for me and everyone. But we must find life's enticements, and they are sufficient to conquer all fear of danger or death and to induce us to be filled with the joy a child feels when he embarks on an expedition with his little friends.

Why must we experience broken partnerships? I see no benefit in doing so, and God knows I have not learned anything because of them. Still, my reflections on these times have dispelled the agitation by which I begin this paragraph. I feel my heart glow with an enthusiasm that elevates me to heaven, for nothing contributes so much to calm my mind as a steady purpose—a point on which the soul may fix its comforting eye except the love I have for my children.

My children captivate my soul, and because of them, every day, I resolve with God to continue with my present undertaking. Am I here to accomplish some great purpose? My life might have not been easy or luxurious, but I prefer my path all the same.

Still with this understanding, my hopes fluctuate. My life has been a difficult voyage that has demanded a sea of fortitude for I feel that I am here to raise the spirits of others when theirs are failing while sustaining my own. I will depart this earth by engaging with my feelings, answering my children's questions to the best of all that I am, and counting my blessings.

I will grow in those blessings, for they are the epitome of who I am and have the key to my soul. I will continue to deem myself as a romantic, nourish my enthusiasm for success and sympathize with those who need my compassion.

Many factors contribute to a satisfying marriage/relationship, such as trust, love, h o n e s t y, c o m m i t m e n t, e x c e l l e n t communication, patience, and respect, to name a few. Honestly, I believe that partnerships in marriage can only begin with a substantial amount of synergy and inspiration.

The dizzying heights of a great collaboration in marriage are empowering, and it makes us ambitious about life as a whole, and the snap crackle and passion of our partnership. Partnerships in the love department pave the way to our spirit. I am delighted to go along with this.

I must close with this: My dreams will continue to be my magnificence and I pray that I will be remembered by all for my courage and for my sympathies which are at my command.

My dearest considerations are my children, my love for God and my efforts to support my trust in him. I ardently desire to maintain a passionate essence for life and to determine my cherished heart.   For you see, the greatest partnership in life is the one that you have with God and your heart.

Epilogue

It is a bit past midnight and I am alone in my house thinking. At this time of night there are few distractions. I don't know about my feelings and thoughts one hundred percent. I am laughing. Perhaps, I am going to go through my entire life thinking I am a rose and find out I am a tulip! The only thing that I know for sure is that I believe in God and His sustaining grace. In a world of changing oyster bars and the technology and the innovation of electric cars, the vanishing news stands and so forth, God is always with me—changes and all. And so, as I bid farewell and close the book on my autobiography, I think about what I have learned and what I can share here with you, that may be helpful. I must give another smile because I have experienced the world, but what have I really learned?

In essence, life can be researched and footnoted, rhymed and narrated, but in the end, I am not sure how much anybody really *knows* about it. I suppose I am a tale of love somewhere, and elsewhere I am a scholar, always learning.

One thing is for sure: We are never too old to learn. Lessons come to us in so many ways. All lessons are worthy of consideration. The strongly-marked surprises in life are learnable moments as well. Don't quarrel about them. A plum tree is a plum tree. If someone sees it differently, let it go.

Arguing is a waste of time. If you are not meant to be with someone, let them go. We are not in this life long enough to be troubled or shame-stricken for that matter. We are all, at some time, ill-judged. It is painful, but dear readers, be cool and confident in all that you do. If you've been wrong in words or actions, apologize right away. Mistakes are part of our human condition. Forgiveness is essential in life, too. Forgiving and forgetting will furnish you with the willingness to move forward. Even though you may not like someone's remarks they are usually better than insults. Do not be a face that just stands in the entrance, walk into life and see what it is all about, but *steel* yourself for the good and bad. Prepare yourself for whatever comes.

The things that loom in life are always there as well as the things that give us joy.

Over-eagerness sometimes can have you trip over life's obstacles, but don't look around so much at everything, because then you won't go anywhere! Difficulties gather around us every single day. Unhappiness comes from not recognizing the rose *and the* tulip. It also comes from not relinquishing ego-centric stumbling blocks in life. One must see the rose and the tulip and not be dispirited. It is up to you to make the earth bloom.

Be generous with your kindness, love and feelings. Let your heart pant and flutter. It is great to be alive! I am Claudia Bannister.

Thank you for reading my life. And remember that Grace from God that sustained me, is available to you.

About the Author

Filled with courage, personality, and a love for God, Claudia Bannister is the accomplished writer and author of *Held By Grace*. By day she works as a Medical Office Administrator. But Ms. Bannister's passion is the women's ministry she founded called, Held By Grace. The mission is to support women on their journey to restoration and alignment of their life purpose.

Born in the Caribbean on the beautiful island of Trinidad and Tobago, she is the mother of two. Widowed at a young age but is passionate about life. Although she has weathered the storms—including divorce and spousal rejection, *Held By Grace* is a story about her life, and God's love.